THE

ANGEL WHO WOULD BE GOD

STEVE BRYAN HUDSON

All proceeds from the sale of this book and all donations received from the distribution of this book will go to the
Building Fund of Mandeville Bible Church
217 Carroll St.
Mandeville, La 70471

THE ANGEL WHO WOULD BE GOD!
©copyright 2024 Steve Bryan Hudson

Scripture quotations taken from the NASB® (New American Standard Bible®), Copyright © 1960, 1971, 1977, 1995, 2020 by The Lockman Foundation. Used by permission. All rights reserved.

ISBN:9798892830898 – Paperback
ISBN:9798892830904 – eBook

Dedication

This book is dedicated to my brother, Parker Hudson,
a man I admire and love.

Contents

Acknowledgments

My thanks and love to my proofreader and foxhole-buddy-for-life, Patsy Hudson, who has been there to support me in every endeavor I pursued.

And, great thanks to the *Encouragers* at Mandeville Bible Church. (You know who you are.) You guys kept me going from chapter to chapter and to the finish line.

Preface

"The only book that should ever be written is one that flows up from the heart, forced out by the inward pressure."— A.W. Tozer

After 45 years of reading, studying, researching, and teaching the Bible, I seem to have acquired an understanding of the "big picture" of God's Word to mankind. Within this understanding, it became clear that some major players in the Bible had specific patterns of behavior. One such player is Satan. My observations about the patterns of this fallen angel originated from what I learned and experienced in my three years of service in the Marine Corps (1970 to 1973).

As a young man, during that period of my life, I attended several schools and training programs with my fellow Marines, some of which focused on strategy and tactics. We studied the enemy of that day, the NVA (North Vietnamese Army) and the Viet Cong (guerrilla units in the South), as well as their tactics. We also studied the significant strategies and tactics used by fighting units in the Second World War and other conflicts. Additionally, we learned about the weaponry, tactics, and strategies employed by small units. Later, I was sent to artillery school to learn my specialty as an "08-02"—the Military Occupational Specialty designation (MOS) of an artillery officer.

The military experience from my early years, combined with the big-picture understanding of the Bible that I gained in subsequent years, gave me a unique perspective of Satan that made for a good study and served as the foundation for this book. I observed that Satan, this brilliant and magnificent creation of God, employed a military-style strategy in his attempt to occupy God's throne in heaven. After Satan's fall to the earth, his strategies and tactics became even more evident as he functioned to defend his position as the *god of this world*.[1]

This book presents the big-picture story of the Bible through a series of significant attacks by Satan on God and humanity. It covers the entirety of the Bible, starting from the angelic creation and fall in Genesis Chapter 1, before time began, to the fall of man in Genesis Chapter 3, and finally, to Satan's ultimate end revealed in Revelation Chapter 20. Past and future history is covered in this book, including the fulfillment of Old and New Testament prophecies that are yet to be completed.

The story is presented in a format that I hope will be engaging for serious Bible students, as well as those with an interest in spiritual matters but have little or no Bible knowledge. Note that this book is not intended to be a commentary, although I do make some comments.

The twenty-two chapters are written in time sequence as the events occur in Scripture. However, each chapter is structured as a stand-alone unit of information and can be used as a Bible lesson.

Satan's attacks on humanity have been continuous from the beginning. He has been on the offensive every moment of every day since his fall; therefore, this book cannot document every single attack. Nevertheless, it highlights the

---

[1] *"And even if our gospel is veiled, it is veiled to those who are perishing, [4] in whose case **the god of this world** has blinded the minds of the unbelieving so that they will not see the light of the gospel of the glory of Christ, who is the image of God"* (2 Corinthians 4:3-4).

major attacks throughout history and prophetic attacks that are still to come.

To Bible scholars and students, kindly read this book with a measure of grace toward the author, depending on your background and understanding of Scripture. You may not agree with the positions taken, hence, the need to extend grace – recognizing that certain suppositions and conclusions were necessary to tell the story.

I hope that as you read this book, you will be blessed in some way by its content.

Steve Bryan Hudson

Chapter 1

⸻⸺◈⸺⸻

The Battle for God's Throne

"The thing worse than rebellion is the thing that causes rebellion."—Frederick Douglass

He was magnificent. This Lucifer[2] was perhaps the greatest and most powerful creation of God. According to the prophetic word of Ezekiel, this angel was an anointed cherub. The cherubim are known for their presence in the throne room and their mission of standing watch to serve their Creator, God. Lucifer, whose name carries the meaning "Light of the Morning Star," was stamped with God's seal of perfection. It is a beautiful name and reveals the obvious affection that God had for this creature.

The prophet Ezekiel uses precious gems known for their beauty and value to describe the esteemed state of this angel:

> *Every precious stone was your covering: The ruby, the topaz and the diamond; The beryl, the onyx and the jasper; The lapis lazuli, the turquoise and the emerald; And the gold, the workmanship of your settings and sockets, was in you.* (Ezekiel 12:13)

---

[2] "Lucifer" is one of the names of the angel we commonly refer to as Satan. It appears that the name "Lucifer" was the original name given to him by God. The name "Satan" is as much a descriptor and identifier as it is a name. The name "Satan" means "Deceiver."

Lucifer was a member of an exalted class of angels known as cherubim – the angels that serve in the throne room of God night and day. By serving God in His inner chamber, he would have the opportunity to observe the attributes of God at every moment. By definition, the *OMNI* characteristics[3] can only describe the Most High God. These powerful and unique qualities would have been seen and somewhat understood by a creature so brilliant in mind and spirit as this angel of light. Lucifer would have witnessed the seraphim flying, circling the throne and heard the resounding voices declaring the holiness of the Most High as detailed by the prophet Isaiah:

> *Seraphim were standing above Him, each having six wings: with two each covered his face, and with two each covered his feet, and with two each flew. And one called out to another and said, "Holy, Holy, Holy, is the Lord of armies. The whole earth is full of His glory." And the foundations of the thresholds trembled at the voice of him who called out, while the temple was filling with smoke.* (Isaiah 6:2-4)

The glory that emanated from the throne of God,[4] His Shekinah

---

[3] Omnipresent, Omniscient, and Omnipotent are but three of the perfect attributes that are given to God alone. That He is All-Present, All-Science (Knowing), and All-Powerful, mutually excludes all other beings from sharing these attributes and His glory.

[4] The throne of God is said to exist in the third heaven, the highest heaven, the place where the angels abide. It is in this location that God calls Satan to give an account of himself (Job 1:6-7). It is in the third heaven that Isaiah envisioned or witnessed the seraphim flying and exalting the holiness of God (Isaiah 6:2-4). The first heaven is the earth's atmosphere. The second heaven is what we identify as "space" – the location of the sun, moon, and planets.

Glory,[5] as well as the incomprehensible majesty of the Triune Godhead,[6] would have been Lucifer's to behold.

He would have observed, known, and worshipped the Son in His pre-incarnate state and identified Him as One with God. Lucifer would have also known the presence, Oneness, and equality of the Holy Spirit. With intellect far more advanced than any human, Lucifer would have understood far better than man the scope, power, and unfathomable depth of the Three Persons of the Godhead whom he worshipped and served.

There is only one God, but Lucifer was just one among the myriad of the angelic hosts that were created—part of the angelic creation that included an innumerable quantity of these spirit beings. While Scripture gives a numerical calculation of this creation, the formula "10,000 times 10,000" is allegorical, indicating a number beyond comprehension.[7]

---

[5] When God, who is spirit, wishes to make His presence known to man, He will appear in a glorious, visible form: as fire or in a cloud, often in combination with a sound such as a strong wind.

[6] God, who is One, has revealed Himself to mankind as having three Persons. This scriptural revelation of the three persons, co-equal in power and glory, is referred to by believers as the Trinity. New Testament passages identify this understanding of the Trinity as God or the Godhead. See Colossians 2:9 in the King James Version of the Bible for the use of the term, "Godhead."

[7] Based upon Jesus' statement in Matthew 18:10, "*See that you do not look down on one of these little ones; for I say to you that **their angels in heaven** continually see the face of My Father who is in heaven,*" some have theorized that there are as many angels as there are people who have been born into the world from the beginning of time—a *guardian* angel for every child. This theory would put the number of the total angelic host above 50 billion. Whatever the number, we know that Lucifer was only one of this enormous quantity of heavenly spirit beings that were created.

15

How long Lucifer served in the throne room of God before leading the great rebellion in heaven is also unknown. Time, as we understand it, did not commence until after Genesis 1:1, which records the creation with the words "In the beginning." The eternal God exists and functions beyond the constraints of time and space. What is known is that the angelic host was present at the laying of the foundation of the earth.[8] Depending on when the accounting of time began, Lucifer's faithful service in the glorious heights of God's majesty may have spanned the equivalent of thousands or millions of earth years. Yet, with all his knowledge of God and his elevated position of service, we meet "The First Rebel." The rebellion began with Lucifer—it ignited in his heart.

A rebellion is the formation of open opposition against the rule of an individual or government. Typically, it is caused by the overbearing rule of a leader or system of control that the masses deem inequitable, tyrannical, or both. In response, they rise up under the leadership of a member of the group to oppose and overthrow the tyrant.

What would it have taken to elicit the support of the angelic host of heaven? What message did Lucifer contrive to pique the interest of the population to even consider his offer? What lies would have been told about the benevolent and Holy God? Given the superhuman intellect of the angels,[9]

---

[8] The Most High God declares to Job that the angelic host ("the sons of God") were present at the creation of the earth. The book of Job declares, *"Where were you when I laid the foundation of the earth? Tell Me, if you have understanding, who set its measurements? Since you know. Or who stretched the measuring line over it? On what were its bases sunk? Or who laid its cornerstone, when the morning stars sang together, and all the __sons of God__ shouted for joy?"* (Job 38:4-7).

[9] While the level of the intelligence of angels is unknown, the implication in Scripture is that it is far above that of humans. First Peter 1:12 tells us

this angelic rebel organizer had to use every new, evil tool in his arsenal.

Since Lucifer was among the greatest, if not the greatest, of God's creation, he would certainly have commanded the respect of the angelic community. Additionally, having served within the "inner circle" of the throne room of God, Lucifer would have had access to information about the Sovereign Lord, and perhaps even His plans. This dynamic and majestic angel would surely have demanded a listening audience among his brethren and used his influential position to stir up thoughts of rebellion.

All rebellions have an objective. Most of them are enacted for the benefit of the masses that rebel against authority. However, this rebellion against the benevolent and holy Most High God was solely for one person: Lucifer. His "I will..." statements declare that the objective was entirely self-oriented. It was for his glory, his elevation, and his throne that the supporting angels sacrificed their exalted positions with God.

Since Scripture doesn't provide us with the details, it cannot be known at what point Lucifer, whom God declared perfect, became imperfect and corrupt of heart. What is known is that it was the admiration of his own beauty, intelligence, and position that moved this incredible creature to sin. Isaiah[10] clearly identified pride as the cause of Lucifer's corruption,

---

that the gospel was "preached to you by the Holy Spirit – things into which angels long to look." This passage, as well as others (such as Matthew 24:36, in which Jesus states that not even the angels know the time of His coming), suggests that angels possess a high degree of intelligence and knowledge.

[10] Isaiah 14:12-15

and it was pride that motivated him to make these statements:

- ***I will*** *ascend to heaven!*
- *Above the stars of God,* ***I will*** *set my throne on high!*
- ***I will*** *ascend above the heights of the clouds!*
- ***I will*** *make myself like the Most High!*

Here is recorded the first sin, the initial act of rebellion of a creature against his Creator. Here is the first instance where the servant creature said to the Master Creator, "Not Thy will, but mine be done!"

The epitome of the proverb, "*Pride goes before disaster, and a haughty spirit before a fall*"[11] finds no better example than that of Lucifer. The wonders of the third heaven, where he served within God's inner circle, surpass human imagination. Just as one is left speechless viewing the second heaven through the lenses of the Hubble and Webb telescopes, the third heaven must be even more indescribable.

This is the environment and position that Lucifer turned his back on in his quest for an impossible equality with the Creator. He sought to ascend above the second heaven, from where he could view the sun and all of the stars and planets.

> *O sun, to tell thee how I hate thy beams that bring to my remembrance from what state I fell, how glorious once above thy sphere.*[12]

Pride is a horrific motivator. It can trigger an irrational

---

[11] Proverbs 16:18
[12] Milton, John. "Paradise Lost Quotes." Goodreads, 2024. https://www.goodreads.com/work/quotes/1031493-paradise-lost

overvaluation of self while causing a severe devaluation of an opponent. Pride impaired Lucifer's judgment, leading him to believe that even when outnumbered two to one, his angelic forces[13] could defeat the angels that remained holy and loyal to God. It was pride that told him he could out-strategize the omniscient God. It was pride that caused him to believe he could overpower the all-powerful God.

With this complete miscalculation, the battle for God's throne was lost. Lucifer, thereafter identified as Satan, was cast from the third heaven (which stood above all the billions of galaxies of the second heaven, each galaxy containing billions of planets and stars) to the singular blue planet known as Earth. His army, comprising one-third of the angelic host, now fallen with Satan, was ejected with him. These fallen angels, often identified in Scripture as demons or evil spirits, would now serve their new master within the confines of Earth and its atmosphere.[14]

Earth – God's creation. Man – God's creation in His image. Man – the authority of Earth. Man – now hated by Satan. How long would Satan serve under the authority of man?

> *The coming of their secret Foe, and scaped, haply so scaped, his mortal snare! For now Satan, now first inflamed with rage, came down, the tempter, ere the accuser, of mankind, To wreak on innocent frail Man his loss of that first battle, and his flight to Hell.*[15]

---

[13] Revelation 12:4 indicates that one-third of the angelic host rebelled with Lucifer, leaving two untainted, holy angels for every evil one that bought into Lucifer's program.

[14] In Ephesians 2:2, Satan is also identified in Scripture as "Prince of the Power of the Air," indicating his realm within the first heaven (atmosphere) of Earth.

[15] Milton, John, *Paradise Lost, Book IV [The Argument],* Poets.org, 2024, https://poets.org/poem/paradise-lost-book-iv-argument

Chapter 2

The Battle for Dominion of Earth

"The supreme art of war is to subdue the enemy without fighting."—Sun Tzu, The Art of War

It was over far too soon. The battle for dominion of the earth was won without a shot being fired. It was bloodless, won by the reigning authority, surrendering dominion with absolutely no resistance. There was no show of force, no challenge, no battle—not even a small skirmish. In fact, not a harsh word was uttered. The white flag was raised by the commander of the earth so quickly that one wonders what the motivating factor was to take such an extreme action as total surrender.

It took incredible genius to accomplish this victory, to achieve triumph without a fight. The victor must have been a masterful tactician to gain the day without setting foot on the field of battle.

Adam, with full knowledge, handed over the domain to his opponent. There were no illusions, no smoke screens. None were needed as he wasn't tricked.

> *And it was **not Adam** who was deceived.* (1 Timothy 2:14)

The tactic used by Satan was to infiltrate and capture. This tactic has been used very effectively through the years, particularly by terrorist organizations. On October 7, 2023, the terrorist organization known as Hamas infiltrated the border that separates the people who self-identify as Palestinians from the people of the nation of Israel. After slaughtering, raping, and murdering hundreds of innocent people at a desert concert and in nearby kibbutzim, the Hamas terrorists proceeded to round up other Israelis, taking them as hostages into Gaza.

Taking hostages puts the aggressor-captor in a decidedly advantageous position when it comes time to negotiate a peaceful settlement. Hamas restrained themselves from slaughtering all of the Israeli victims in order to retain bargaining chips for the negotiating table. It is always an effective move because it inflicts virtually intolerable pain and heartache on the captives' loved ones. The intense suffering imposed upon the families causes such an emotional upheaval that the internal pressure seeks immediate relief.

This, then, is the strategy: infiltrate and take a hostage. Then, use the hostage as the pressure point to gain victory. Satan is the ultimate terrorist to mankind and is the author of the horror, pain, and pressure caused by hostage-taking. In this first conflict with humanity, it was Satan who took the first hostage. Her name was Eve.

There are basically two different versions of what took place. Some commentators and Bible narrators contend that both Adam and Eve were present when the Fall took place. The couple were together when Satan appeared to them in the garden. They both listened to the beguiling words of the talking snake that were directed toward Eve. When she was convinced, she ate the forbidden fruit, then passed it to Adam who bit into the sinful act.

If this version is correct, then why would Adam, who was not deceived but saw through the serpent's misinformation, stand by while watching Eve risk her life by consuming the fruit forbidden by God? This version seems to be based on two words added to Genesis 3:6, correctly translated by the New American Standard Bible (NASB):

> **NASB (correct translation)** *"When the woman saw that the tree was good for food, and that it was a delight to the eyes, and that the tree was desirable to make one wise, she took some of its fruit and ate; and she also gave some to her husband with her, and he ate."*

> **NIV (incorrect translation)** *"When the woman saw that the fruit of the tree was good for food and pleasing to the eye, and also desirable for gaining wisdom, she took some and ate it. She also gave some to her husband, <u>who was</u> with her, and he ate it."*

An article entitled, "Genesis 3 – The Fall – Why Did Adam Sin?" records the discrepancy and the correct understanding of the verse:

> *Many modern translations promote the erroneous interpretation of Adam being present during the Serpent's temptation of Eve by supplying two English words that are not included in the Hebrew narrative: "**who was**." The Hebrew merely says she "also gave unto her husband with her." The errant translations say Eve gave to "her husband **who was** with her." Rather than providing an accurate translation, the addition of these words is interpretive in nature. This false translation leads readers to an inaccurate understanding of what happened.*

> *While this is not an exhaustive list, the ESV, HCSB, ISV, NET, NIV, and NRSV are among the English*

> *translations that inappropriately add the words, "who was". The KJV, NASB, and NKJV accurately translate the passage without them.[16]*

The other far more plausible version (and closer to the meaning of the text), shows the events of Genesis Chapter 3 happening sequentially: Eve first, and then some undefined time later, Adam. The initial event depicts Eve alone, isolated. Yet, Eve was not the ultimate target of Satan. It was Adam. Why? Because Adam was the person to whom God had delegated dominion of the earth. This transfer of authority took place in Genesis Chapter 2 with the placing of the man in the garden and the naming of the animals by the man, all prior to the creation of the woman. It was Adam who held the position of authority,[17] and it was Adam who had to be defeated by Satan in order to assume control of the earthly domain.

Pride was always, and continues to be, the root corruptor of Satan. This highest creation of the angelic host was cast down to Earth because of his pride, and now, he had to dwell on the earth. How could the magnificent Lucifer, the Morning

---

[16] "Genesis 3 – The Fall – Why did Adam Sin?", Revealed Truth, 2024, https://www.revealedtruth.com/bible-study/genesis3-adam-sin-fall/

[17] That Adam had the authority to control the domain of Earth can be clearly seen during the testing of Jesus in the wilderness. We see the third, and final, temptation of Jesus by Satan. "*Again, the devil took him to a very high mountain and showed him **all the kingdoms of the world** and their splendor. '**All this I will give you**,' he said, 'if you will bow down and worship me'*" (Matthew 4:8-9).

The authority over the domain of the earth passed from Adam to Satan when Adam willfully disobeyed God through the pressure applied by Satan. From this point forward, Satan assumed the role of *Domini* – headmaster and controller of the earth. Had Satan made the offer that he proposed to Jesus without substantive authority, He would have rebuked him in response. Yet, Jesus did not contest the substance, legitimacy, or authority of this offer by Satan.

Star, the Bearer of Light live on the earth under the authority of a man? Control must be wrestled from the hands of this Adam.

You were in Eden, the garden of God. (Ezekiel 28:13)

Satan was already very familiar with the garden of Eden. Scripture places him there prior to the fall. He knew the territory well. One of the factors that favors an infantry squad in setting an ambush is knowledge of the terrain. Another factor is knowledge of the habits and weaknesses of the enemy.

Clearly, Satan studied his prey as they walked in the garden with God – man, created in the image of God. One can imagine the fury of the powerful, beautiful, prideful fallen angel as he watched Adam being created on the very territory that was Satan's exiled home. Then God gave this first man full authority over the territory. Adam was given dominion over the earth. While Satan and the angelic host were created as holy, spiritual creatures with enormous power and intelligence, it was man whom God loved. Satan's primary enemy was God, and it was Adam, this created image of God walking in the garden with God, enjoying intimate fellowship with God, that became enemy #1a of his.

Then, a second creature, like man, but different, appeared – a creature also bearing the image of God. Satan studied both of them carefully and intently. It didn't take long for him to comprehend that this creature was incredibly precious to Adam. In fact, it was blatantly obvious that this woman, derived from man, was more valuable to Adam than all of the animals God created to be under Adam's authority.

The question then became: is this the weak spot? Is this the avenue of approach to victory? Is this woman more precious to Adam than God?

Leave it to Satan to turn God's good provisions into tools for evil. If this woman is Adam's most prized possession, then she is the path to victory.

The man's soft underbelly was the woman! With Adam's potential vulnerability exposed, Satan developed his tactics. This battle had to be won in two steps. The first would be to isolate the woman, take advantage of her lack of knowledge of the garden[18] or other perceived weaknesses, and get her to willfully disobey God's instruction to Adam. Her disobedience would then create disharmony in the woman's relationship with the man. Once the tension was created, it would then be up to this man, Adam, to choose how to resolve the issue.

> *Birds rising in flight is a sign that the enemy is lying in ambush; when the wild animals are startled and flee he is trying to take you unaware.*—Sun Tzu

> *Now the serpent was more cunning than any animal of the field which the Lord God had made. And he said to the woman.* (Genesis 3:1)

---

[18] Scripture does not comment on the extent of Eve's knowledge of her environment before the temptation. It does appear that Adam benefitted from the close relationship with God, as well as his understanding of the animals. It was Adam, before Eve's arrival, who walked with God in the garden and was introduced to the animals. He had sufficient understanding of their characteristics to name them. This is not to say that Eve was not at fault for her willful act of sin. However, her lack of understanding may have made her a more vulnerable target.

It is clear from the normal flow of the text in Scripture that Eve was alone, isolated. Adam, it appears from the reading, would have spotted the trap. We don't know why or how Eve was alone, but we do know that through the cunning of Satan (personified by the description of the serpent), the ambush was set. Again, the words were not harsh; the tone was not aggressive. In fact, the talking serpent[19] seemed downright helpful—advising and implying that Eve was not getting the most out of her relationship with God. Note in the conversation below how Satan carves Adam out of the scenario he proposes. Eve speaks of *we* (herself and Adam), while Satan uses the individual term, *you*. One wonders how Eve perceived this offer and whether it included Adam.

> *The woman said to the serpent, "From the fruit of the trees of the garden we may eat;* [3] *but from the fruit of the tree which is in the middle of the garden, God has said, 'You shall not eat from it or touch it, or you will die.'"* [4] *The serpent said to the woman, "You certainly will not die!* [5] *For God knows that on the day you eat from it your eyes will be opened, and you will [a]become like God, knowing good and evil."* (Genesis 3:2-5)

From here, we know that Eve made a major blunder. She evaluated the offer based on Satan's words and her own perception (It looks good, sounds good; it'll improve my position.), and ate the fruit. Neither her relationship with God nor Adam was taken into account in her decision.

---

[19] Some have suggested that Eve would have been protected by Adam had the two been together. This certainly seems logical given that Adam had more intimate knowledge of the animals (a talking snake?), as well as a deeper relationship with God that was established before Eve's creation. Yet, Eve is certainly not blameless. She could have relied upon Adam's counsel before eating the fruit. And, of course, like Adam, she had total access to God.

> *And it was not Adam who was deceived, but the woman was deceived and* **became a wrongdoer**. (1 Timothy 2:14)

Mission accomplished. The first part of the battle plan was successfully completed. The woman became a wrongdoer—the first sinner created in God's image. Eve willfully submitted to Satan's instruction and surrendered the best that God had given her—her position of holiness. She exchanged it for an evil heart. Now, she was in the perfect position to be manipulated by Satan and used to confront the man.

The second part of the plan required no effort on Satan's part, for the woman did exactly as he had predicted. She had eaten the fruit forbidden by God. She did not die, but something changed. Something was wrong. The perfect, spotless, cherished mate of Adam lost something—although at this point, she did not comprehend its meaning. Eve only knew that she no longer matched the sanctity of her beloved mate. She was different, and he was not.

Now, it was up to Eve to reestablish the equilibrium that would reconnect her with Adam. The problem was, she could not eliminate the disparity. She could no longer reach his height. There was only one way.

> *And she also gave some to her husband with her.* (Genesis 3:6)

The choice was presented to Adam. His most cherished possession, Eve, had been tainted, and his perfection would not allow him to unite with the one who had made him complete. She was his completion, his wholeness. Adam was not deceived by the offer made to Eve; that was not his motivation. He saw right through the total misrepresentation that the talking snake made of God. While Eve desired to be like

God, equal to God, as God, Adam did not share this desire. His longing was to restore union with Eve. The dilemma now lay before him: obey his Creator or follow Eve so that the two could be equally tainted.

With the forbidden fruit consumed, Adam willfully rebelled against God and simultaneously surrendered his dominion authority to the spirit behind the serpent. Satan had become the god of this world (2 Corinthians 4:4), and from this point onward, the whole world lay under the power of the Evil One (1 John 5:19).

No shot was fired and no words were spoken. Adam surrendered. The creature had become more important to Adam than the Creator.

Chapter 3

The Aftermath – Mopping Up

"The war has ruined us for everything."—Erich Maria Remarque, *All Quiet on the Western Front*

Death was everywhere. Such was the aftermath of so significant a battle.

Death. But there were no bodies, no bloody remnants, no destroyed tanks, howitzers, or any other implements of a recent battle to be found on the battlefield.

No, the death Adam suffered in his bloodless defeat was of the spiritual kind. He and Eve remembered what God had told them: "On the day that you eat thereof, you shall surely die." They ate, and both were still alive. But not like before. Everything changed. The animals—those wonderful, friendly creatures of God that so easily came to Adam to be named—now avoided his presence at the sound of his footsteps. These warm companions that once easily mixed with him and Eve, and each other, were now hunting and killing, and being hunted and killed. Physical death entered the earth. Nothing, and no one was safe.

Adam, the P.O.W. of Satan, was now under the government of his conqueror. Adam's world had a new god.[20] Adam was

---

[20] *"Satan, who is **the god of this world**, has blinded the minds of those who don't believe"* (2 Corinthians 4:4). **Note:** While the Apostle Paul identifies Satan as the god of this world, he was not sovereign. Numerous

subjugated to Satan in the way that conquered people exist under the auspices of a new, ruling master. And just as the child of a slave becomes the property of the slave's owner, so too would Adam's offspring belong to Adam's ruler. Adam's spiritual death would be passed down to every child born of his seed. With the knowledge of good and evil acquired by Adam from eating the fruit came the understanding that he wasn't designed to handle this knowledge. This death wrought by Satan changed Adam's spiritual DNA such that every offspring of his would possess their forefather's fallen nature. That nature would seek to satisfy the offspring's own selfish desires, causing the person to lean toward Satan and away from God. Because Adam's offspring would be born with his newly corrupted nature, every person born from the seed of Adam would be hostile toward God. No longer was mankind given open access to fellowship with God as Adam had in the garden. Without some method of resolving this hostility, there could be no fellowship with Him.[21]

God had judged and pronounced a curse upon Eve, as well as Adam, and even upon the ground itself. All of creation felt the weight of the awful decision.[22] Day-to-day life,

---

passages in the Bible demonstrate limits on Satan's authority and position. He is still subject to appearing before God, on demand, and accounting for his actions. Satan is still limited to what he may do under God's authority (Job 1:6-12).

[21] *"For the mind set on the flesh is death, but the mind set on the Spirit is life and peace, [7] because the mind set on the flesh is* **hostile toward God***; for it does not subject itself to the law of God, for it is not even able to do so, [8] and those who are in the flesh cannot please God"* (Romans 8:6-8).

[22] *"For we know that the whole creation groans and suffers the pains of childbirth together until now"* (Romans 8:22).

which had been so very easy became so very difficult. Work, which had always been so enjoyable, suddenly became burdensome. Even the wonderful, intense, and satisfying relationship the man had with the woman was now tainted. Adam's leadership suddenly became difficult. Before, it went smoothly, without effort, and was greatly appreciated by his wife. Now, with the curse, Eve resented Adam's headship.

While this was a day of doom for Adam, his wife, and his future offspring, it was not doomsday for humanity. It was not the end for man, but it was the beginning of the end for Satan who was also brought before God. At this time, God announced "The Rescue Plan" for Adam and his race.[23] God's rescue plan had been prepared to reconcile Adam, Eve, and all future generations to Himself. When He announced the components of His plan, He sounded the death knell for Satan. There were five major parts of God's plan.

- There will be a Rescuer—a man.
- The Rescuer will spring from the woman's "seed," not from the seed of man.
- The Rescuer will be an enemy of Satan and those who belong to him.
- Satan will wound the Rescuer—through the heel—but the wound will not be terminal.
- In the end, the Rescuer will crush Satan with a head wound that will ultimately be terminal.

While this plan had just been revealed, it wasn't a new one. God, in His omniscience, had prepared His plan to rescue Adam's race,

---

[23] *"And I will make enemies of you and the woman, and of your offspring and her seed; He shall crush your head, and you shall bruise Him on the heel"* (Genesis 3:15).

even before Adam was created.[24] Thus, Satan was put on notice that the war he started had not ended—it had only just begun. Although he had usurped Adam's headship over the earth and brought down Adam's world, Satan's victory was only temporary. In the end, his reign over the earth had a terminal point. Satan would be overthrown by an offspring of the woman without man's involvement. She alone would provide the "seed" that would bring forth the great Rescuer of Adam and his race.

Satan was the newly minted *god of this world*. However, he was now forewarned that his title was in jeopardy. The forewarning of a coming Rescuer meant that Satan had to defend his position. He realized he had to conduct and initiate future campaigns and win battles against God and His Rescuer to protect his new godship.

"Make them believe, that offensive operations, often times, is the surest, if not the only (in some cases) means of defense."—George Washington, 1799

Washington meant that the best defense is a good offense. Washington was right. It was a proven strategy. Satan developed this tactic long before George Washington's time.

To defend his position as *god of this world*, Satan quickly prepared to go on the offensive.

Attacking God and mankind will be his best defense.

---

[24] *"Just as He chose us in Him **before the foundation of the world**, that we would be holy and blameless before Him* (Ephesians 1:4). The sovereignty of God is clearly on display in this passage, planning for a solution to save people from His wrath even before the creation."

Chapter 4

———····◁∞▷····———

The Seed-Kill Campaign

The Assassin

"The important thing to know about an assassination is not who fired the shot, but who paid for the bullet."—Eric Ambler

In military terms, a campaign is a broad strategy that typically takes a long time to complete and covers a wide geographic area. Campaigns may encompass numerous subordinate operations and maneuvers, often leading to multiple battles and skirmishes.

In the Pacific Theater of World War II, the United States Navy, led by Admiral Chester Nimitz, conducted the Island-Hopping Campaign against Japan. In this campaign, Marine invasion forces were ferried from island to island by a fleet of ships. These forces then launched amphibious assaults to locate and destroy the Japanese forces occupying each island. The Japanese airstrips on these islands were subsequently repaired, upgraded, and converted to accommodate American Navy and Marine planes. These aircraft supported the "hop" to the next Japanese-held island and controlled the shipping lanes between the islands. This campaign required complex operations and brutal battles to advance toward the enemy's mainland. Some of the island-taking operations within the Island-Hopping Campaign included these well-documented conflicts:

- Battle for Guadalcanal

- Battle for Tarawa
- Battle for Peleliu
- Battle for Iwo Jima
- Battle for Okinawa

In a similar strategic move, while not knowing Satan's plans for a long-term operation against God's provision to rescue Adam's race, it appears from history that the Devil was prepared for multiple encounters to protect his new kingdom. Included in his strategy was an ongoing campaign against the unknown "seed of the woman."[25]

Not all encounters in war involve direct battles between large opposing forces. Some behind-the-scenes conflicts among a few participants can determine the outcome of nations. One of the significant small-scale conflicts in history that helped shape world events involved two brothers. To suggest that Satan was not involved in this conflict would be to ignore his ability to influence one or both parties.

> *And Satan stood up against Israel, and provoked David[26] to number Israel.* (1 Chronicles 21:1)

If the offspring of the woman was destined to lead the rescue mission that would destroy Satan and free Adam and his

---

[25] God's curse upon Satan in the garden after the fall of man included the prophecy that the descendant, or seed, of a woman, would one day inflict him with a mortal wound that would crush his head. See Genesis 3:15.

[26] While Satan is not directly or indirectly involved in every evil decision of mankind, we can certainly reference Scripture to link him to the first taking of a human life. Jesus speaks to the Pharisees in John 8:44: "*You belong to your father the devil and you willingly carry out your father's desires. He was a murderer from the beginning.*" This was the first murder (from the beginning) and was one that launched Satan's campaign to crush the seed of the woman.

offspring, then the seed must be crushed at all costs. In the Seed-Kill campaign, Satan will use both covert and overt tactics to eliminate the offspring of the woman whom God had declared would lead to Satan's ultimate defeat and loss of power. If this seed can be destroyed, then the government of Satan and his lordship and position as *god of this world*[27] will be eternal.

The first action of Satan was covert in nature. He knew these three facts from God's pronouncement regarding the rescue mission that would destroy his regime:

1. A human, not an angel, would be the Rescuer.
2. This human would be a male.
3. This human would be of the seed of a woman, not of a man.

It is not surprising, then, that Satan watched Eve with a predator's eye as she and Adam's family grew.

The first offspring of the woman and her husband was Cain. Since the command was to be fruitful and multiply, Scripture implies that soon after, a second male was born to the couple—Abel. It appears that at this point, the family was limited to two males (It would not be until Adam was 130 years old that the next male offspring was born.) and certainly, a number of females.[28] One of these two male children would either be the seed of the woman that God spoke of or possess

---

[27] *"And even if our gospel is veiled, it is veiled to those who are perishing, 4 in whose case* **the god of this world** *has blinded the minds of the unbelieving so that they will not see the light of the gospel of the glory of Christ, who is the image of God"* (2 Corinthians 4:3-4).

[28] These female births answer the question, "Where did Cain's wife come from?" Cain married one of his sisters.

the spiritual genetics of the righteous line to pass on to the next generation. The solution for Satan was obvious: eliminate the offspring who was the conduit God planned to use to fulfill His promise.

There were two issues that needed to be addressed. One was to identify the son who would carry the righteous lineage. The second issue would be to develop the approach to eliminate that son. The first was relatively easy to overcome. The second, not so much.

The story of Cain and Abel as presented in books, television, and movies often portrays Abel as the quiet, pensive, nice, fair-haired son. Cain, on the other hand, has an evil look about him. A dark demeanor accompanies this sinister aura that Cain displays and the spiritual gap between the two young men is palpable. The message is clear: Cain is the evil one, and Abel is the innocent, nice guy. However, it wasn't that simple to discern between the two because both were sinners.

> *Behold, I was brought forth in guilt, and in sin my mother conceived me.* (Psalm 51:5)

The Bible doesn't specify the demeanor or general behavior of either young man. What is clear is that both of Adam's children were sinners. Both needed to bring sacrifices. After all, they were conceived in sin following the fall of Adam and Eve and their parents' subsequent expulsion from the garden where they walked with God. Both Cain and Abel possessed the sinful nature inherited from their father—a fallen part of all people, regardless of nationality, background, environment, or race that inclines humanity toward sin. What we find in the very limited information on Cain and Abel is that both brought sacrifices to God, evidencing that they sought reconciliation with God through the sacrifices.[29]

Satan knew that the very first sacrifice was a bloody transaction. He saw the animal skin that God used to clothe Adam and Eve and knew the requirement of God for a substitutionary sacrifice for sin. Satan knew because he was present with newly-sinful Adam and his equally sinful wife when this first killing of an animal happened!

Satan observed the sacrifices of both of Eve's sons. It was apparent to him which of the two would carry the righteous lineage. Scripture quickly distinguishes between Cain and Abel based on the sacrifices they brought before the Lord. Abel offered the best blood sacrifice he could offer and did so with a right heart toward God. In contrast, Cain brought an offering of produce from his very own field, accompanied by an attitude of obstinance. Even when God tried to counsel Cain and guide him into a righteous relationship, Cain showed only resentment and rejected God's guidance.

> Jesus speaking to the Jews validates the righteousness of Abel: ... *so that upon you will fall the guilt of all the righteous blood shed on earth, from the blood of **righteous Abel** to the blood of Zechariah, the son of Berechiah, whom you murdered between the temple and the altar.* (Matthew 23:35)

From Satan's observations, it was clear that Abel had received God's gift of righteousness through his faith, submitting himself and his sacrifice to God according to the Lord's

---

[29] *"And the Lord God made garments of skin for Adam and his wife, and clothed them"* (Genesis 3:21). Only after the fall of man did the sacrificial system begin. It was introduced to humanity when God took the life of an animal to provide clothing for the shamed Adam and Eve.

prescribed approach. Abel belonged to God; Cain did not. Cain's sacrifice was rejected by God. This angry young man also rejected God's counsel to enter a relationship with Him.

This conclusion was easily determined after observing both boys and their interactions with God. Now, however, the second issue arose, which was far more complex for Satan. Despite being the ruler of this world, Satan was not sovereign. It is not specifically stated in Scripture, but it seems that Satan had no authority to take a believer's life unless he first received permission from God.[30] In order to eliminate the righteous Abel, the work had to be done by another. Satan now moved one of his powerful chess pieces into position. Cain, his knight, would make the attack that would kill the righteous seed of the woman.[31]

It was Cain who fired the weapon, but Satan provided the bullet. While Cain vented his rage by murdering his brother, it was Satan who declared himself the victor of this conflict. In a small-scale assassination, Satan destroyed the lineage of

---

[30] When God was challenged by Satan regarding Job's faithfulness, Satan required God's acceptance of the challenge to take away the many blessings He had given him. However, God's acceptance limited the authority when He told Satan, *"Behold, all that he has is in your power; only **do not reach out and put your hand on him**"* (Job 1:12).

We also see this limitation of Satan in 1 Corinthians 5:5, where Paul instructs the church, *"Deliver this man to Satan for the destruction of his flesh, so that his spirit may be saved on the day of the Lord."* It is only with the removal of God's protective hand on the life of this man that Satan can physically harm him.

[31] That Cain was acting under the influence of Satan is revealed in 1 John 3:11-12, *"For this is the message you have heard from the beginning: we should love one another, [12] unlike **Cain who belonged to the evil one and slaughtered his brother**. Why did he slaughter him? Because his own works were evil, and those of his brother righteous."*

the future Rescuer of Adam's race, who was supposed to crush the head of the serpent.

"The thrill of victory must have lasted quite a while because it wasn't until Cain's murderous work was offset by the birth announcement—probably over 100 years later[32]—when Eve shouted, "I have a new baby boy!""

So, it wasn't over after all. God thwarted Satan's work by raising up another man to carry the seed of the righteous line. This new man-child, Seth, replaced Abel as the carrier of the seed that would one day launch God's rescue mission.[33] Satan's simple and quick assassination attempt to guarantee his eternal reign on Earth had failed.

A new approach had to be devised for Satan's next offensive action in the Seed-Kill Campaign.

---

[32] If Cain and Abel were young men under 30 years old when the murder took place, it would be over 100 years before Seth was born. *"Adam was one hundred and thirty years old when he begot a son in his likeness, after his image; and he named him Seth"* (Genesis 5:3).

[33] *"Adam again had intercourse with his wife, and she gave birth to a son whom she called Seth. 'God has granted me another offspring **in place of Abel**,'" she said, 'because Cain killed him'"* (Genesis 4:25).

Chapter 5

—·⋅⟨∞⟩⋅·—

The Seed-Kill Campaign

Hacking the Code

"The power of biological weapons is ten times more than the nuclear power. Unless we act fast with an open mind, any one of them can extinct the human race."—Amit Ray, *Nuclear Weapons Free World – Peace on Earth*

With the setback from the failure of Abel's assassination to snuff out the righteous line, it was time for Satan to launch an attack using his special operations troops. If the murder of the specific seed did not work, then a wider-scale operation would be used to halt the progress of God's rescue plan. After Seth's birth, it apparently didn't take long for Satan to put his next operation into action to destroy the seed of the righteous line.

Otto Skorzeny was a high-ranking special operations commando of the Waffen SS in Hitler's Third Reich in 1944. Skorzeny gained fame and favor within the German high command because of the successful operation he had conducted the previous year. This commando mission resulted in the successful snatching of Benito Mussolini, a personal friend and an important ally of Hitler, from his Italian captors after the overthrow of Mussolini's dictatorship. Because of this successful, high-risk retrieval of Mussolini, Skorzeny was said to be one of Hitler's favorites in the German Waffen SS.

After the D-Day Landing, which began the Allied invasion

of Europe, Hitler planned a massive counterattack against the American and British forces. This counterattack became known to American forces as the "Battle of the Bulge." Part of Hitler's plan included sending English-speaking German soldiers, outfitted as GIs and driving captured American jeeps and tanks, ahead of his counterattacking panzer troops. The following letter from Hitler to Skorzeny reveals Hitler's clandestine game plan.

> *I want you to command a group of American and British troops and get them across the Meuse and seize one of the bridges. Not, my dear Skorzeny, real Americans or British. I want you to create special units wearing American and British uniforms. They will travel in captured Allied tanks. Think of the confusion you could cause! I envisage a whole string of false orders which will upset communications and attack morale.*[34]

The fact that the mission given to him by Hitler violated the laws of the Geneva Convention regarding impersonating the opposition's forces—emulating their dress, language, and personality—was no obstacle for Skorzeny. Success at all costs for the glory of the Führer was easily justifiable.

Hitler wasn't the first to employ this deceptive tactic of cloaking his troops to integrate them with the opposition for nefarious purposes. Like many of his evil "firsts," Satan originated this concept. He wanted to send his "troops" on a mission "clothed" as those he was attacking to become a part

---

[34] Butler, Rupert, (1979). *The Black Angels*. New York: St. Martin's Press. p. 183–184.

of the people he sought to eliminate. That his demons[35] could take on appearances as humans should not be surprising.

> *Do not neglect to show hospitality to strangers, for by this some have entertained <u>angels without knowing it</u>.* (Hebrews 13:2)

Throughout Scripture, angelic and spirit beings are seen in some physical form. Satan even took on the body of a snake in one instance. God's messengers are often seen as men with full, physical characteristics.[36] Therefore, it is easy to understand that Satan's fallen angels sent on this mission were outfitted with human features. They were able to acquire the physical characteristics of men to carry out their special mission.

But the form that the angels took was less significant than the ultimate objective of their mission. This mission objective was another first of its kind; it was a mission to conduct biological warfare on humanity! Biological weapons, by their nature, are dangerous yet remarkably effective in various ways.

---

[35] Demons are not a special spiritual creation of God. Demons are fallen angels. They are highly intelligent and very powerful spirit beings, possessing the same functional attributes of the angels who did not rebel. The word "demon" is a transliteration of the Greek word *daimon,* which referred to intelligent, god-like beings of mythology.

[36] In Genesis 18:1-12 the angels that visited Abraham were seen by him as three men. In Genesis Chapter 19, two of these three men went into Sodom and Gomorrah; yet, the Bible identified them as angels. These angels had all of the physical attributes of a human male and performed human functions that angels do not need to do such as eat and drink.

Biological weapons may be employed in various ways to gain a strategic or tactical advantage over the enemy, either by threats or by actual deployments. Like some chemical weapons, biological weapons may also be useful as area denial weapons. These agents may be lethal or non-lethal, and may be targeted against a single individual, a group of people, or even an entire population.[37]

The effectiveness of bio-weapons was brought to the forefront of the world in October 2018. A "Breaking News" announcement by the television anchor during the evening national news put the inhabitants of Earth on notice. A biological germ had escaped from a laboratory in China and was beginning to infect the local townspeople at an alarming rate. This germ, identified as COVID-19, was designed to attack the human (biological system), making it a man-made biological weapon. However, this weapon was far from the first. History reveals the use of biological weapons over the centuries as seen in the following table[38]:

Examples of biological warfare during the past millennium[39]

Year	Event
1155	Emperor Barbarossa poisons water wells with human bodies – Tortona, Italy

---

[37] *Biological Warfare.* Wikipedia.org. Retrieved May 15, 2024, from https://en.wikipedia.org/wiki/Biological_warfare

[38] *The History of Biological Warfare.* Retrieved May 12, 2024, from https://www.ncbi.nlm.nih.gov/pmc/articles/PMC1326439/

[39] *The History of Biological Warfare*, Friedrich Frischknecht, EMBO Reports, June 2003

Year Event

1346 Mongols catapult bodies of plague victims over the city walls of Caffa – Crimean Peninsula

1495 Spanish mix wine with blood of leprosy patients to sell to their French foes – Naples, Italy

1650 Polish fire saliva from rabid dogs toward their enemies

1675 First deal between German and French forces not to use "poison bullets"

1763 British distribute blankets from smallpox patients to Native Americans

1797 Napoleon floods the plains around Mantua, Italy, to enhance the spread of malaria

1863 Confederates sell clothing from yellow fever and smallpox patients to Union troops

A review of the examples shown in the previous table, when compared with those of the 21st century (including the manufacture of deadly viruses such as COVID-19), shows how sophisticated humanity has become. But long before mankind used weapons to attack the human biological system, Satan had developed an incredibly complex biological attack strategy to destroy humanity and, in doing so, eliminate the righteous line.

In the beginning of Adam's race, a man took one woman as a wife in marriage.[40] This one-to-one union continued until the fifth generation of Cain, at which point Scripture highlights that a man named Lamech boasted of taking not just

---

[40] Jesus, when responding to the question of divorcing one wife and taking another said, *"In the beginning it was not this way"* (Matthew 19:8).

one, but two wives.[41] Counting the generations from Adam in years, it would be close to 130 years that Lamech (Cain's fifth generation offspring) introduced polygamy. This time frame matches the age of Adam (130 years) when Seth was born to Adam and Eve (Genesis 5:4-5). This may be the time the Bible refers to when "mankind began to multiply on the earth."[42] It was at this time when human multiplication began, and polygamy was introduced that we see Satan's supernatural biological attack on the generations of humanity.

> *The sons of God saw that the daughters of mankind were beautiful; and they took wives for themselves, whomever they chose.* (Genesis 6:2)

The plan was simple. The battalion of fallen angels with human characteristics (identified as "sons of God") were to take women (identified as the "daughters of mankind") to procreate with them. These troops ignored the norm of arranged marriages of a man to a woman to form a family unit, which was God's plan. Instead, each demon had sexual intercourse with as many women[43] as he chose. Unlike the targeted assassination of Abel to eliminate the righteous line through which the Leader of the Rescue Mission would come, this action was designed to produce mass "casualties."

The casualties would be a woman impregnated with a demonic seed that hacked the human DNA code and modified

---

[41] "*Lamech took two wives for himself: the name of the one was Adah, and the name of the other, Zillah*" (Genesis 4:19).

[42] "*Now it came about, when mankind began to multiply on the face of the land, and daughters were born to them*" (Genesis 6:1).

[43] The Bible is very clear in describing the sexual act between the demon and the women in Genesis 6:4, "*When the sons of God came in to the daughters of mankind, and they bore children to them.*" See also: the Author's Comments at the end of this chapter.

it. These demon-children, born from the ungodly union between a spirit being taking on human male physical characteristics and a fully human woman, would grow to become extraordinary people. When matured, they would have capabilities that far exceeded those resulting from a normal union between husband and wife.

The Bible records such an offspring:

> *The* **Nephilim** (Hebrew word for "**giants**") *were on the earth in those days, and also afterward, when the sons of God came in to the daughters of mankind, and they bore children to them. Those were the* **mighty men** *who were of old,* **men of renown**. (Genesis 6:4)

In altering the biology of humans, Satan attempted to produce a Super Race. As seen in Scripture, these men of might would take any woman they desired. There was a sense that taking by force would certainly be an available option given their strength and overall superiority. There is every reason to believe that the Nephilim were also superior in intellect, since they were the offspring of angels who are far superior to mankind in both physical and intellectual capacities. Eventually, this Super Race would dominate by absorbing all women and overpowering all normal children produced. Only evil, genetically modified humans would exist. The result: no righteous line, no "seed of the woman," and God's plan thwarted. Satan would retain his kingdom.

The impact on infected humanity from this demonic biological attack was immediate. The depth and breadth of the corruption impacted humanity to such an extent that however evil man had become due to Adam's sin, followed by Cain's sin, this interaction with fallen angels was far worse. This wasn't just one sin by one man that had to be dealt with. No. This was a weapon of mass destruction. The downward trajectory of mankind was drastically changed from a sinful path to a satanic nosedive of self-destruction comparable to a flaming Japanese kamikaze bent on death, destruction, and immolation.

> *Then the LORD saw that the wickedness of mankind was great on the earth, and that every intent of the thoughts of their hearts was only evil continually.* (Genesis 6:5)

The great Creator, who with an unseen display of power spoke such a magnificent creature as man into existence, was hurt to His core. The love of the Creator for mankind was matched only by the power that created him. Yet, man displayed "only evil continually." Satan, the most beautiful and powerful of all God's creations, had taken what God loved and cared for, and turned them into a fallen race so corrupt and evil that it grieved God to His core. Satan's hatred of God could not have been more evident than in this vicious act against the Fatherly God, for what father would not be deeply hurt by a child turned to evil.

> *Then the Lord said, "I will wipe out mankind whom I have created from the face of the land; mankind, and animals as well, and crawling things, and the birds of the sky. For I am sorry that I have made them."* (Genesis 6:7)

Unlike the assassination plot to wipe out the righteous line where God waited 100+ years before providing Seth as the carrier of Abel's lineage, God responded quickly.

AUTHOR'S COMMENT: There are two views among Bible students regarding the intercourse involving the sons of God and the daughters of men spoken of in Genesis 6:4. The first view identifies the sons of God as the offspring of Seth and the daughters of men as the offspring of Cain. This interpretation sees the mixing of these two human lineages as Satan's attempt to eliminate the righteous line (holy) of Seth with the evil unholy lineage of Cain. The rationale for this approach is that angels are sexless and therefore cannot engage in sexual intercourse as described in Genesis 6:4. The problem with this view is that it cannot account for the horrific offspring that was produced from the union of two normal human beings.

The second view, which this author subscribes to, identifies the sons of God as angels, specifically fallen angels. Nowhere in the Old Testament is humanity described using the term "sons of God," whereas we see that same term is exclusively used in the Old Testament to describe angels – as is seen in Job 1:6, where God calls these angels, including Satan, into account.

> *Now there was a day when the **sons of God** came to present themselves before the Lord, and <u>Satan also came among them</u>.*

One author states that the term, "Nephilim," in the original Hebrew means "creatures – half men and half demons, who were born of the horrible rebellion of the demons."[44]

That angels cannot have sexual intercourse is a principle taken from Jesus' comment to the Sadducees regarding marriage in heaven in Matthew 22:30.

---

[44] Barnhouse, D. (1970). *Genesis* (p. 48). Zondervan Publishing Company, Grand Rapids, MI.

> *For in the resurrection they neither marry nor are given in marriage, but are like angels in heaven.*

But this passage in Matthew does not specify that angels cannot engage in sexual activity.

It appears, by using all of Scripture to decipher the meaning of Genesis 6:4, that a significant group of fallen angels had entered the physical universe in a manner that was a gross violation of God's allowance for their continued freedom. Jude speaks of angels who left the dimension or domain that God had provided and that these angels actively participated in some form of sexual activity with human flesh.

> *And angels who did not keep their own domain* **but abandoned their proper dwelling place**, *these He has kept in eternal restraints under darkness for the judgment of the great day, just as Sodom and Gomorrah and the cities around them, since they in the same way as these* **angels indulged in sexual perversion** *and went after* **strange flesh**, *are exhibited as an example in undergoing the punishment of eternal fire.* (Jude 1:6-7)

The question remains: how could these angels have sexual intercourse with women? Scripture does not provide a definitive answer regarding the mechanics of the act; it simply states that the act occurred and resulted in a horrifically mutated offspring.

Chapter 6

The Sovereign Judge

"There is not a square inch in the whole domain of our human existence over which Christ, Who is Sovereign over all, does not cry, "Mine!""—Abraham Kuyper

Satan had his way. Evil begot evil. Satan's "boys" did their part of intermixing with humanity, and the biblical record indicates that humanity loved it. This is not surprising. The human heart is fundamentally evil.[45] Inside of man is that inherent, inherited desire to lean toward darkness and to flirt with sin. But this sin was not merely flirted with—humanity dove in headfirst! It led to degradation of the worst order. Ultimately, mankind was stuck in the muck of spiritual and moral corruption, feeling hopeless.

When all was lost, the Sovereign Lord interceded in the affairs of men. The seemingly dormant, long-suffering God of all was at last roused from His throne. It was the fallen angels of Satan's troops who mounted an attack of sexual perversion against mankind that initiated His response. The evil aftermath spurred His follow-through. The initial swarm of evil angels invaded a dimension they were prohibited from entering at the time of Seth's birth. This led to the proliferation of the demon seed throughout mankind, spreading from

---

[45] *"The **heart is deceitful above all things**, and **desperately wicked**: who can know it? I the LORD search the heart, I try the reins, even to give every man according to his ways, and according to the fruit of his doings"* (Jeremiah 17:9-10).

parent to child and onward for over 1500 years across the earth. The by-product of the infection was astounding, as is stated: *"Then the LORD saw that the wickedness of mankind was great on the earth."*[46] The breadth of the spread was equally catastrophic. Virtually all of humanity was caught up in the increasingly corrupt and decrepit cesspool that was once God's spotless creation.

The stench from the horrible condition of the earth reached His throne. There was no creature above the powerful Satan that could intervene and put an end to the degradation that had taken place. At this point, the Creator raised His hand and cried, "Mine!" as if to call off all others as He caught the plummeting earth. It was His, alone, to deal with. And deal with it He did. The first execution of His judgment involved the angelic creation:

> *And angels who did not keep their own domain but abandoned their proper dwelling place, these He has kept in eternal restraints under darkness for the judgment of the great day, just as Sodom and Gomorrah and the cities around them, since they in the same way as these angels indulged in sexual perversion and went after strange flesh, are exhibited as an example in undergoing the punishment of eternal fire.* (Jude 1:6-7)

There is a facility in a location and dimension unknown to man that serves as the most awful of detention compounds. Where it exists is unknown, but its name is recognized: Tartarus, a place of darkness and dread. The name Tartarus is of Greek mythological origin. It was the absolute worst place in the afterlife, where extremely evil people, and even monsters were sentenced, according to Greek mythology. If not

---

[46] Genesis 6:5

worse than hell, it was considered the lowest level of hell, characterized by darkness and torment. The term Tartarus appears only once in the New Testament, where it is often translated as "hell." Second Peter Chapter 2 refers to the same event documented in Jude 1:6-7 (above) but specifically identifies the name of the angels' imprisonment.

> *For if God did not spare angels when they sinned, but cast them into hell (Tartarus) and committed them to pits of darkness, held for judgment.* (2 Peter 2:4)

It is in Tartarus, in this dimension of the underworld humanity cannot perceive, that these violators of their "first estate" were sent. The passage in Jude concerning these demons states that they were kept in chains (eternal restraints) so they could not escape to return to the estate i.e., the dimension of humans. In Revelation, this place is further defined as the abyss, a bottomless pit. There is a shaft that descends to this pit of oblivion, and it is kept under lock and key. It is a smoldering place filled with snarling demons whose fury must be contained to protect humanity from the further evil they would inflict upon the creation made in God's image.

The second judgment of the Sovereign was the total destruction of man and all living creatures on Earth.[47] Perhaps God thought that it was better to start with a clean slate—kill every living thing.

---

[47] Even in a world-wide, full scale nuclear holocaust, it is estimated that at least 1 percent of the world's population would survive. People living in remote locations, on distant islands and in areas that are far removed from any significant population would likely live through the destruction. But God, and only God, could scrub the earth clean of all living creatures.

But, in the execution of that judgment, this most significant pronouncement was made. Humanity would survive.

> *Noah found grace*[48] *in the eyes of the Lord.* (Genesis 6:8)

It is important to note that it was through eight people (Noah, his wife, their three sons, and three daughters-in-law) that humanity would continue to exist. It is even more important to note that of these eight people, all were sinners. All had been judged. All would have been killed as a result of God's judgment of total destruction. But, as is written, "*Noah found grace in the eyes of the Lord!*"

Noah was the man whom God declared to be righteous. Perfect? No. Noah was a sinner, and like all sinners, he was judged inadequate when compared to God's standard of holiness required of all people. Yet, God said that Noah was righteous.

> *Noah was a righteous man, blameless in his generation. Noah walked with God.* (Genesis 6:9)

Noah was declared by God to be righteous because he was a man of faith.[49] Noah believed what God said and he followed His Word, trusting in it. He is said to have "walked with God." Noah was blameless, not because he was perfect and free from sin, but because God covers and pays for the sins of His righteous ones.

---

[48] Grace is unearned favor or merit.

[49] "*By faith Noah, being warned by God about things not yet seen, in reverence prepared an ark for the salvation of his household, by which he condemned the world, and became an heir of the righteousness which is according to faith*" (Hebrews 11:7).

This righteous man also carried the righteous seed because he was of the line of Seth. Had God proceeded with His judgment in destroying all humanity, the righteous line would have also been terminated. Satan's plan would have been successful, and God's pronouncement that the seed of the woman would crush Satan's head would have been doomed to fail.

There was only one path to survival through the coming flood: God's path, which was the covering provided by the ark. Noah was tasked to build this floating shelter to God's exact specifications. By following God's specific plan, the burden of salvation was placed not on Noah, but on God Himself! The ark, a floating shelter, protected eight sinners from the wrath of God upon sinful mankind. On that boat rested the hope of mankind: complete trust in God, total dependence on His design. Total faith to cut the first log and to drive the first nail. Noah's work was the byproduct of faith, and faith was the byproduct of grace. This grace is the foundation upon which God would rebuild mankind.

AUTHOR'S COMMENT: The Nephilim (giants produced by the demon seed) were destroyed along with all of humanity, except the eight sinners on the ark. However, the question must be raised: did the demon seed somehow survive alongside the righteous seed-of-the-woman that ran through Noah's blood?

Almost 1,000 years after the flood, when the children of Israel were led by Moses into the land of Canaan, spies were sent into the land to scope out the terrain and the opposition. The terrifying report that they carried back with them was recorded in Scripture.

> *So they brought a bad report of the land which they had*
> *spied out to the sons of Israel, saying, "The land through*
> *which we have gone to spy out is a land that devours its*
> *inhabitants; and all the people whom we saw in it are*

people of great stature. [33] ***We also saw the Nephilim there*** *(the sons of Anak are part of the Nephilim); and* <u>*we were like grasshoppers*</u> *in our own sight, and so we were in their sight.* " (Numbers 13:32-33)

If these giants (and, later, Goliath and his brothers) were identified by Scripture as Nephilim, then they were of the same hybrid race produced before the flood.

There are two possible explanations that may account for the post-flood Nephilim.

1. One of the people on board the ark carried a dormant gene of the hybrid race while not displaying any of the characteristics. Tracing the genealogy upward from the people of Caanan who occupied the land of Caanan (which is where the Nephilim lived) the line of the Canaanites begins with Ham and his wife. It would seem possible that Ham's wife retained the genetic mutation that could produce a "rebirth" of the Nephilim.

2. Or, a second and smaller *wave* of demons decided to follow the first group that went after strange flesh and they impregnated a new number of the daughters of men. Anak (see Numbers 13:33) may have been the first of the new line of Nephilim, and other giants were born to his wives.

The Bible does not comment on what happened that caused the Nephilim to reappear. It does seem that while they did return to occupy a place on the earth, the impact, scope, and breadth of their presence was limited to the land of Canaan until they were eventually killed off.[50]

---

[50] After the Israelites began to take possession of the Promised Land, the old man of faith, Caleb, requested that the mountain containing the giants (Anakim) be given to him so he could drive them out. See Joshua 14:12.

Chapter 7

Fort Beelzebub

"You gotta love the names. They're so eager, earnest, and hopeful: Camp Prosperity, Camp Liberty, and Camp Victory are the names of just a few of the U.S. military bases in Baghdad."—Richard Engel

After the comprehensive destructive "progress" that Satan made by using his demons to inseminate the daughters of men, the righteous line made it through the fray. Although Noah and his sons did the construction work, it was always God's ark, not man's. The ark is such a picture of the grace of God. This buoyant, steering-less, seemingly directionless watercraft ensured the continuation of the righteous line through Noah. The Seed-of-the-Woman lineage would one day produce the Rescuer promised by God. God's judgment and wrath were poured out on the earth, consuming the Super Race of giants, all humanity, and all the animals outside of His ark. However, Noah found shelter in this enclosed, protected, and safe floating vessel because "Noah found grace in the eyes of God."

Satan is a spirit being and from the time of his ejection from heaven to the earth, he operated throughout the spiritual realm. He had attempted to bridge the physical gap to control the earth by generating a quasi-physical presence using his demons, fathering a Super Race. But God had scrubbed the earth and cleansed it of Satan's monstrosity. With the disappearance of the Nephilim, Satan changed course. His new approach to influence the physical realm was to establish a base of operations—a physical property—from which he could direct his forces. This new headquarters would serve as the launching point for an entirely new plan of attack, operating in conjunction with the Seed-Kill Campaign. But first, he needed a <u>human</u> general[51] to run his earthly headquarters.

In the meantime, God pronounced His blessing upon the tiny remnant of the flood. It was through these four couples that the rapid repopulation of the earth would begin.

> *Then God blessed Noah and his sons, and said to them, "Be fruitful and multiply, and fill the earth."* (Genesis 9:1)

Even with the blessing from God, it didn't take long for the first sin of the new beginning to be recorded. Noah, this preacher of righteousness, the one who found grace in God's sight, drank himself into unconsciousness,[52] followed immediately by his youngest son's sin of gross disrespect for his drunken father. Satan saw the sin of the youngest son, Ham, and it was just the opening he was looking for. The problem was that Ham didn't have the power to pull off what Satan

---

[51] Satan already had an upper echelon of spiritual generals. These demons were cast down to the earth with him after the heavenly rebellion failed. Only one of them, General Abaddon, was not available because he was in chains in the abyss. General Abaddon led the mission of the "sons of God" to impregnate the "daughters of men," and his punishment for leading the attack was the same as the other demons who took part. Scripture tells us that Abaddon is currently a prisoner in the abyss and that he rules over all the demons in that hellhole. *"They have as king over them, the angel of the abyss; his name in Hebrew is Abaddon, and in the Greek, he has the name Apollyon"* (Revelation 9:11).

[52] Even the "Great Men of Faith" fall short of God's standard. God, who is rich in grace and mercy awaits the sinner who seeks His face, desiring to reestablish fellowship.

needed and neither did Ham's son Cush, so Satan waited patiently. It was in Ham's grandson, Cush's son, when the population began to explode, that Satan identified his man. His name was Nimrod. If Satan could have fathered a son, it would be Nimrod. People would then say of the son, "The apple didn't fall very far from the tree. He's just like his dad."

> *Now Cush fathered Nimrod; he became a <u>mighty one</u> on the earth. [9] He was a <u>mighty hunter</u> before the Lord; therefore it is said, "Like Nimrod a mighty hunter before the Lord."* (Genesis 10:8-9)

This Nimrod was a mighty one, the first person the Bible records as having superior strength before the Lord. He was a powerful man. He hunted, and the Bible doesn't say that he just hunted animals. This guy was a warrior and a feared killer. Nimrod had personal physical strength, along with a strong personality. Plus, he had a charismatic charm. Nimrod knew how to lead people, and they were attracted to him like a magnet drawing flecks of metal. People always seek out the strong one to follow—the person who will give them an inner sense of peace and security.

Nimrod was the First Article. People who supply the military know what a first article is. Each U.S. military soldier, sailor, marine, and airman is equipped with the absolute best weaponry, clothing, food, and other government issued support. Prior to the issuance of a purchase order to acquire a helmet, a rifle, a bullet, or rations, a prospective supplier is provided stringent specifications under which the product is sold to the U.S. DoD (Department of Defense). The supplier's product must be manufactured to meet or exceed these specifications. The supplier then prepares a small sample of the product offering that was produced under the specifications and this sample, called the First Article, is tested and reviewed by the DoD. If it is accepted, the DoD issues a large production order with the requirement that all the items produced must replicate the First Article.

When it comes to "Satan's Man," Nimrod was the First Article. It could be said that this man, hand-picked by Satan, was the first *antichrist*. Like the antichrist who will appear thousands of years later, Nimrod was a *type*.[53] He epitomized the man, the human, who will one day appear and be the antithesis of all the Son of God is. He will oppose all that is God's desire for mankind. That is the antichrist, and Nimrod was his forerunner.

What Satan loved was that Nimrod was a man full of pride, just like him. Humble people kneel before the Lord. Not Nimrod. You would never see him on his knees before God. In fact, his attitude of rebellion invoked a saying among the people, which they liked to broadcast to show their admiration of his prideful attitude toward the Creator. They said, "Like Nimrod, a mighty hunter before the Lord." Nimrod drew Satan's attention as the ideal man to spearhead his weapons of diversion.

One more thing: Nimrod was a king—the first king on Earth recorded in Scripture. His might, physical presence, overpowering personality, planning capabilities, and organizing and executive skills put him on top of humanity in those early years after the flood. This man was the driving force behind the acquisition of territory in Shinar, where four major cities were built under his reign: Babel, Erech, Accad, and Calneh. He then expanded his kingdom by conquering or acquiring territory in Assyria where he duplicated his work in Shinar and built four more cities: Nineveh, Rehoboth-

---

[53] Isaac was presented as a sacrifice on the altar by his father, Joseph was rejected by his brothers, and even the innocent lamb offered as a sacrifice, were all *types*, or previews, of the coming Savior.

Ir, Calah, and Resen.[54] With the acquisition of territory and the completion of eight major construction projects, Nimrod had built a kingdom for his personal glory. He was a self-made man, a natural leader, a killer, and a king who stood in opposition to God. Nimrod was a man after Satan's own heart.

It was one of the cities built by Nimrod – Babel – that Satan chose to be his headquarters—with Nimrod as his commanding general. Babel became a city-state (a self-governing entity typically led by a king) known as Babylon in the land of Shinar. The name is a derivation of *babilu,* which means, "gate of god."[55] There is further meaning to the name Babylon from Hebrew writers:

> *The name is derived by the Hebrews from the root "balal" ("to confound") and has further reference to the confusion of tongues at the Tower (Gen 11:9). Thus, the Biblical writer refutes any God-honoring connotation of the name.[56]*

The city-state of Babylon was small in size and population, but it would become an empire. Kings, such as Hammurabi and Nebuchadnezzar will occupy the throne of the Babylonian empire in Nimrod's future. Each king will expand the reaches of his kingdom by conquering surrounding territories,

---

[54] *"And the beginning of his kingdom was [e]Babel, Erech, Accad, and Calneh, in the land of Shinar. [11] From that land he went to Assyria, and built Nineveh, Rehoboth-Ir, Calah, [12] and Resen between Nineveh and Calah; that is the great city"* (Genesis 10:10-12).

[55] Unger, M. F. (1957). *Unger's Bible Dictionary* (3rd ed., p. 115). Moody Press, Chicago, Il.

[56] Ibid.

as well as defeating kingdoms that sought to gain key land acquisitions.[57]

> *And on her forehead was written a name of mystery:*
> *"Babylon the great, mother of prostitutes and of*
> *earth's abominations."* (Revelation 17:5)

As the power and control of the Chaldean rulers (the people of Babylon) spread, the empire became known as "Babylon the Great!" The influence of this empire infected other nations far and wide, including that of the nation and people of Israel. Babylon's empire took on a personality, much like an American city today that has become known for its sinister atmosphere. New Orleans' Bourbon Street carries with it an advertisement for drunken immorality as does Las Vegas, where a traveler can participate in illicit behavior and retain anonymity – *What happens in Vegas stays in Vegas.*

The empire of Babylon will become touted as one of the great ruling entities of the world. Nebuchadnezzar, the great king of Babylon, had a dream of a statue with a head of gold, a chest of silver, a midsection of bronze, and two legs of iron. Because he couldn't understand the dream's significance, a young Jew captive by the name of Daniel was called by the king to interpret the meaning. Daniel, the young prophet, revealed that Babylon was seen as the "Gold Standard" of evil empires that would rule the world, and Nebuchadnezzar was at the height of the statue as king of kings—but, only under the sovereignty of God.[58]

---

[57] *"And the king of Egypt did not come again out of his land, for the king of Babylon had taken all that belonged to the king of Egypt from the Brook of Egypt to the river Euphrates"* (2 Kings 24:7).

[58] *"You, O king, are the king of kings, to whom the God of heaven has given the kingdom, the power, the strength, and the honor; and wherever the sons of mankind live, or the animals of the field, or the birds of the*

This same Babylon will become one of the heads of the seven-headed dragon of Revelation, representing Satan's manipulation of human governments throughout the ages that will precede the eighth and final world government of the antichrist.[59]

> *At the time John was writing in A.D. 90, five of these world powers had fallen – Egypt, Assyria, Babylon, Medo-Persia, and Greece. During the time of the Apostle John, Rome was the world power and so fits the description "one is." The seventh world power would refer to the final confederation during the Tribulation out of which comes the eighth – the Antichrist.[60]*

If Nimrod was the First Article of a rebellious, powerful man, then Babylon had to be his headquarters because it stood as the land of defiance to all that God deemed holy and righteous. The writers of Scripture from Genesis to Revelation viewed this city as sinful. The prophets of old spoke of Babylon's sexual immorality and its evil commercial practices. Babylon is referred to 280 times in the Bible,[61]

---

sky, He has handed them over to you and has made you ruler over them all. You are the head of gold" (Daniel 2:37).

[59] *"And they are seven kings; five have fallen, one is, the other has not yet come; and when he comes, he must remain a little while. The beast which was, and is not, is himself also an eighth and is one of the seven, and he goes to destruction"* (Revelation 17:10-11).

[60] Epp, T. H. (1969). *Practical Studies in Revelation, Vol II*. The Good News Broadcasting Association, Inc., Lincoln, Ne. p. 311

[61] Zavada, J. (2019, December 4). *Biblical History of Ancient Babylone*. Learn Religions. Retrieved May 5, 2024, from https://www.learnreligions.com/history-of-babylon-3867031

associating the city and its people with sin, rebelliousness, and power. Babylon, with Nimrod on its throne, was destined to become the beacon of Satan's dark message to the ancient world.

Fort Beelzebub was in business and ready for action.

Chapter 8

⸻⸺∞⸻⸻

The Diversion

"As a diversion, few things were as effective as chocolate cake."— Louise Penny, *The Madness of Crowds*

L ouise Penny was right. When dealing with kids, chocolate cake can distract them from whatever their eyes are focused on. A good diversion comes in handy.

Satan had lost the first two battles of the Seed-Kill Campaign. The work of Cain, the assassin, was defeated by God with the birth of Seth to continue the righteous line. Moreover, the Super Race that the "sons of God" had hoped would overtake the earth was wiped out by the scrubbing of the earth from the flood. The Seed-Kill Campaign was not yet deemed a failure, even though it did not achieve short-term success in either of the battles. A campaign's success cannot be determined by just one or two battles when more are to come. Setbacks and losses in battles happen to most generals in the course of a war. The campaign can only be judged by the ultimate outcome of the planned objective: to kill the carriers of the righteous line, thereby destroying the seed. This was paramount in Satan's plan. That strategy had to continue. More battles had to be fought by Satan to prevent this righteous Leader from one day being born from the seed-of-the-woman. The Seed-Kill campaign had to continue and plans for future battles had to be drawn by Satan.

Satan had to play the long game. Because of the two early losses, it became apparent that this campaign to kill the seed would be drawn out over time. While he was moving his chess pieces toward the next battle in the campaign, mankind would grow from the eight people on the ark. These humans would multiply quickly to populate the earth. Satan had to act fast. He needed to divert the attention of this new off-spring of humanity in order to maintain his position as the *god of this world*, while the primary mission to eliminate the righteous seed continued. It was time to implement a diversionary strategy.

> *The eye is diverted from the real business, it is caught by the spectacular action that means nothing--nothing at all.*—Agatha Christie

A diversionary strategy is often used in wartime. The objective is to misrepresent the intention of the attacking forces or to bluff the enemy into not recognizing the main thrust of the attack. Prior to the D-Day invasion of Europe that would hit the beaches of Normandy, the United States Army created a diversion to distract the Nazi generals with what became known as the Ghost Army. The concept was to use this intentional misrepresentation of combat forces to keep the German high command guessing concerning the deployment of US troops. The Ghost Army wasn't a real army, but it sure looked and sounded like one. The 23rd HQ Special Troops was comprised of barely over 1000 soldiers and officers designed to portray two army divisions of 15,000 men each, along with the full array of their supporting mechanized units.

> *Armed with nothing heavier than .50 caliber machine guns, the 23rd took part in 22 large-scale deceptions in Europe from Normandy to the Rhine River, the bulk of the unit arriving in England in May 1944, shortly before D-Day. The brainchild of Colonel Billy Harris and Major Ralph Ingersoll, both*

American military planners based in London, the unit consisted of a carefully selected group of artists, engineers, professional soldiers, and draftees, including famed artists such as fashion designer Bill Blass, painter Ellsworth Kelly, and photographer Art Kane. Many West Point graduates and former Army Specialized Training Program participants were assigned to the 23rd, and it was said to have one of the highest IQs in the Army with an average of 119. The unit waged war with inflatable tanks and vehicles, fake radio traffic, sound effects, and even phony generals, using imagination and illusion to trick the enemy while saving thousands of lives along the way. The 23rd, along with the 3133rd Signal Service Company in Italy, helped liberate Europe from the grip of Nazi tyranny.[62]

Tanks and armored personnel carriers, as well as mobile artillery batteries, were all fabricated—not of steel, but of rubber. The façade of this army is particularly noteworthy since it consisted of inflatable tanks and other heavy-appearing machinery and weaponry that could be moved rapidly and with ease. It all looked so real to the German aerial reconnaissance analysts who were assigned the task of tracking troop movements. The Ghost Army was a full-scale distortion of the real deal—imitation bait that was readily taken and consumed.

Like this fabrication army, the misrepresentation that Satan presented to "Humanity-Part 2" was even more effective. His bait was gladly taken in place of the original because the

---

[62] *Ghost Army: The Combat Con Artists of World War II*. National WWII Museum. Retrieved May 9, 2024, from https://www.nationalww2museum.org/visit/exhibits/traveling-exhibits/ghost-army-combat-con-artists-world-war-ii

imitation appealed to the fallen nature of this new iteration that proceeded from the survivors of the great flood. Shortly after the remnant of eight set foot on dry ground and left the ark to begin life anew in this strange new world, God immediately acted by blessing the four couples and gave them the following command:

> *Then God blessed Noah and his sons, and said to them, "Be fruitful and multiply, and **fill the earth**."* (Genesis 9:1)

It was God's design for those who found grace, those who made it through the cleansing flood that reestablished and renewed the earth, to **fill the earth**. The people who were to spring forth from the four couples were instructed by God to spread out and take possession of the land that God had cleansed. But thanks to General & King Nimrod, the rebellion began immediately, followed by the great diversion:

> *Then they said to one another, "Come, let's make bricks and fire them thoroughly." And they used brick for stone, and they used tar for mortar. ⁴ And they said, "Come, let's build ourselves a city, and a tower whose top will reach into heaven, and let's make a name for ourselves; otherwise we will be scattered abroad over the face of all the earth."* (Genesis 11:3-4)

No one said Nimrod wasn't smart. He was very smart, and he was an organizer and a leader—he was Satan's man, after all. With this new technology that these people developed using fabricated brick for stone and tar to keep the bricks cemented, Nimrod directed the construction of ... you guessed it! ... Babylon. The action unified the people as never before. They were instilled with pride. "Let's make **a name for ourselves**," shouted King Nimrod, "this city will keep us together and prevent us from being scattered all over the place, like God wants."

Oh, one more little tidbit is revealed in this act of rebellion recorded in Genesis—and herein is the diversion: "Let's build ourselves a city, and **a tower whose top will reach into heaven.**"

The tower that Nimrod was talking about became known as, "The Tower of Babel." It became the focal point of the rebellion because it was aimed at God in heaven. It was to show Him that these people were independent of Him and refused to follow His rule. But, more than this, the tower became the first temple. It was the first recorded, "high place" that was used by the people of their day. In fact, it is the very first instance of paganism recorded in the Bible. Throughout all the pre-flood activities of man, there is no record of any false deity or any form of worship other than that toward God. But now, we have the introduction of Satan's diversionary tactic: paganism. Now, Satan has implanted a method of keeping people under his thumb. He makes them focus on worshipping their way, whatever and whoever they want – as long as it is not the worship of God – particularly the worship of God as He instructed!

Soon, these tower-buildings that reached the high places were being erected in all of Nimrod's kingdom.[63] Satan's pagan system of worship encouraged polytheism, the worship of many gods, and pantheism, the worship of the earth and things of nature. Statues and images were created and erected in these temples to reach their self-created versions

---

[63] These temples were known as ziggurats. A ziggurat is an ancient Mesopotamian temple tower consisting of a lofty pyramidal structure built in successive stages with outside staircases and a shrine at the top.
See: https://www.merriam-webster.com/dictionary/ziggurat

of deity. Idolatry and false religions followed. Of particular note in this array of false worship is the errant concept of a tower that would allow man to reach God his own way. This thought goes all the way back to Cain, for this was his error.[64] Cain thought that he could bypass God's instructions on how He required man to approach Him.

Satan loves religion. He is the great inventor of the concept that we hear in a hamburger chain's commercial: "Have it Your Way!" Find a religion that satisfies you. If you don't like God the way He declares He is, develop your own version of God, and worship Him your way. After all, if you're religious that's all that matters. Heck, you don't even have to be religious—you can take the position that you're good enough—that you're a pretty good person. After all, the good things about you outweigh the sinful things about you, and God will gladly accept you when you stand before Him. Right?

Chalk another one up for Satan's diversion. Unfortunately, at death, all the self-appraised good and religious people who follow a religion that runs counter to God's book, will find themselves in a terrible position that can't be corrected. Satan's diversionary tactic will have taken them down the Yellow Brick Road to destruction.

Satan's diversionary tactic of a "Ghost Army" of idolatry and false religions has run for about 4000 years, and it is still going strong.[65] Human religions have spun off and proliferated

---

[64] See Author's Comment at the end of this chapter.

[65] Like the Ghost Army, a false religious system will look authentic and attractive from afar. Only when examining closely will it be shown to be a façade and not hold up to scrutiny and questions about what it teaches and offers to man.

from this root idea of Nimrod. And, like Satan, people love religions. This diversion that keeps peoples' eyes away from the downward spiral of humanity will stay with mankind for the duration. Religions and idolatry will finally disappear during the end-times. In a brilliant move by Satan, he will merge all religions into one. This One-World ecumenical religion will be incredibly powerful, incredibly rich, and chock-full of idolatry. It will teach the doctrine of demons and misrepresent the person of Jesus Christ. At the same time, it will profess that Jesus was a holy religious leader of His time and His religion is one of the many paths to God and heaven.

When Satan's chosen one (the antichrist) has moved himself into position to take control of the world, the One-World religion will be destroyed by Satan. After all, when Satan's man takes over rulership of the world, declares himself to be God, and demands that all worship him, Satan cannot possibly tolerate idols and false worshippers!

AUTHOR'S COMMENT: Cain was rejected as was the offering to God that was prepared his way instead of following God's instructions. Cain was rejected and so will every person who is determined to approach God on his own terms. Over the thousands of years, formalized religions have emerged, and derivations of these religions have morphed into differential forms of religious organizations that we call cults. Some religions, and even cults, are correctly monotheistic in their doctrine. However, these religions have developed rituals, laws, regulations, and requirements their subjects must follow to please God and have a chance of going to heaven. Some religions teach that God allows man to earn grace by performing certain religious actions or works of "righteousness" – while God's clear specifications are entirely ignored.[66]

Religions are extremely dangerous when their rules, canons, rituals, and instructions depart from the Bible. The Bible is the written Word that comes from God. When a religious directive, policy, doctrine, or law runs in contradiction to the Bible, it is indicative of the very error that Satan introduced through Nimrod and the rebellious people of Babylon. Those who follow these religions that teach earned access to heaven will not be justified by God. They will stand before Him to be judged by their deeds at the Great White Throne of Judgment.[67]

---

[66] Grace, by its very definition in the Bible, is a gift. Grace is free and cannot be earned. It is that free gift of grace that is received by the one who, "believes on Him," that gives eternal life. "*For by grace are you saved, through faith, and that not of yourselves, it is a gift of God*" (Ephesians 2:8-9).

[67] "*Then I saw a great white throne and Him who sat upon it, from whose [g]presence earth and heaven fled, and no place was found for them. 12 And I saw the dead, the great and the small, standing before the throne, and books were opened; and another book was opened, which is the book of life; and the dead were judged from the things which were written in the books, according to their deeds*" (Revelation 20:11-12).

Chapter 9

·····◁∞▷·····

The Seed-Kill Campaign

The Imposter

"I wasn't a Pan Am pilot or any other kind of pilot. I was an imposter."—Frank W. Abagnale *Catch Me If You Can: The True Story of a Real Fake*

It worked! Beautifully! The diversion tactic employed by Satan accomplished everything that he had hoped it would—and more. Idolatry fed humanity's innate desire to worship like nothing else.

Ultimately, it didn't matter to Satan that God interceded in Nimrod's plan to resist the Lord's command to spread out and occupy the earth. When Nimrod dug in to stop the Lord's command from being carried out, the Sovereign God took action to force the people to fill the earth—to follow the command that He had ordered. He divinely introduced new and various languages among all the people, shutting down the massive construction projects designed to unify the population. As people sought to communicate with each other, they formed language groups that left Babylon to find their own land, their own place.

The distribution of languages and dispersion of people to populate the earth was quite alright with Satan. When the people left, they took with them the idols and false religions that had been given birth in Babel (later known as Babylon).

Satan's idolatry spread throughout the earth as the people dispersed.

> *Nimrod established a system of idol worship that detested God and worshiped Satan. God confused their language and scattered them all over the earth and they took this false religious system with them into all the world. Babel later became known as Babylon where all false religions and idol worship came from.*[68]

From the dispersion at the Tower of Babel, Scripture moves forward 350 years and points the reader to a man by the name of Abraham.[69]

> *Now these are the records of the generations of Terah. Terah fathered* **Abram***, Nahor, and Haran; and Haran fathered Lot.* [28] *Haran died during the lifetime of his father Terah in the land of his birth, in* **Ur of the Chaldeans***.* [29] *Abram and Nahor took wives for themselves. The name of* **Abram's wife was Sarai***, and the name of Nahor's wife was Milcah, the daughter of Haran, the father of Milcah and Iscah.* [30] **Sarai was unable to conceive***; she did not have a child.* (Genesis 11:27-30)

It was with Noah, through his son Shem, that God had ordained the righteous line that would carry the seed of the woman destined to crush the head of Satan. In studying the

---

[68] Carlin, L. (2016, August 23). Babylon, the mother of all false religions. *Ag Air Update.*

[69] Before he came to know the One and only God, his name was Abram, which means "exalted father." Later, God will change Abram's name to Abraham, which means "father of many nations."

lineage of Abram back to the flood, the Bible traces his heritage all the way to Shem, the son of Noah. Abram grew up in the land of Ur of the Chaldeans. Ur is located in the region of Shinar, which also contained the city-state of Babylon. The Chaldean people were its occupants. They were the original worshippers of false gods in Ur, where Abram lived. Their deities included:

- Marduk – the dominant god of Babylon (aka Bel)[70]
- Absu – god of the underwater seas
- Sin – the moon god
- Nabu – god of wisdom
- Anu – god of heaven
- Utu – the sun god
- Kishar – god of creation
- Ishtar – the goddess mother
- Tammuz – the son god of Ishtar
- And others …

It might be thought that the lineage carrying the seed of the woman that would crush the head of Satan would be free from Babylonian idolatry. Scripture reveals the opposite. Idolatry was practiced not only among the offspring of Ham and Japheth but also among the descendants of Shem. It appears that idolatry was the universal foundation of religion in this repopulated world. Satan's ghost army of idols was readily worshipped. Humanity substituted counterfeit deities for the glorious deity of the Most High God.

---

[70] Marduk was later known as Bel, a name derived from the Semitic word "baal," or "lord." Bel had all the attributes of Marduk, and his status and cult were much the same. Bel, however, gradually came to be thought of as the god of order and destiny. Encyclopedia Brittanica website, https://www.britannica.com/topic/Marduk

With the entire world following Satan's path to hell by adopting idols to worship, God had to intercede.

> *The willingness to obey every word from God is critical to hearing God speak.*—Henry T. Blackaby, *Hearing God's Voice*

When God intervenes in the affairs of men, His sovereign voice is unmistakable. Satan had no choice but to watch as God made direct contact with His man, Abram. The Most High didn't make the call to this man through a sign, a sooth-sayer, or even a prophet. It was a direct intervention, speaking person-to-person with this man by the name of Abram.

The Creator severed the cords of the evil rope that Satan used to bind this man chosen to carry the seed forward. God's first action was to lead Abram out of the idolatrous hotbed of his hometown of Ur.

Abram was born and raised in the land of the Chaldeans (the people that lived in Babylon), the language group that followed Nimrod and stayed put when the dispersion took place and the people of all other languages departed. This Babylon was the city that drank from, washed clothes and bathed in the water drawn out of the Euphrates River, which passed into and through the city. It is the Euphrates River that will one day release the demons being housed in its waters.[71] God had to get Abram out of this unholy surrounding.

There was no mistaking this voice. Abram heard it, not just in his ears, but throughout his very being. The voice was so

---

[71] During the 6th Trumpet Judgment, which will take place during the Great Tribulation, four demons that have been bound will be released. *"Saying to the sixth angel who had the trumpet, 'Release the four angels who are bound at the great river Euphrates'"* (Revelation 9:14).

powerful that it overwhelmed all Abram had been taught about religion, worship, and gods over the many years he grew up in this land of Ur. "Go to a new place," He said. "Get out of here. Get out of the land that you've known for the past seventy-five years." At a time when men at 75 years of age have laid down their roots, dug in for the duration, built their last house, and started really enjoying life, God said to Abram, "Move on! Leave your security and the protection that comes from being in a clan. Now, move on and leave it all behind."[72]

Didn't this deity know how dangerous it was going to be? Abram would have to pass through territories where people watched him with questioning and suspicious eyes. His clothes and mannerisms would mark him as an outsider—a person not easily welcomed. Abram's small group would be easy pickings for road gangs, killers, and robbers.

Abram was asked to go to a new place—to a land he knew nothing about. The voice didn't tell him what or where the final destination would be. He just had to start going and the voice would tell him when he got to this unknown place that he had arrived. There were no GPS systems. No maps. Not even a seasoned guide to lead him.

Risky? Yes, but there were incentives. God made promises—guarantees. Abram would be unbelievably compensated. The people he was leaving behind, his family, would be replaced with a family that would become, not just another clan, but a great nation! In addition, Abram wouldn't be just another man in the crowd. No! His name would be so well known and spoken of that he would be called "great."

---

[72] This is a paraphrase of God's command to Abram. For the actual communication from God to Abram, see Genesis 12:1-3.

His life would have incredible meaning because every people group in the world would be blessed by him!

One more thing: what about the security from being in a clan that was left behind? Not to worry. Abram and his family would be blessed by other people and nations because this new God would bless them for blessing him and his people. This God would also ensure that those who oppose Abram will be cursed.

> *So Abram went away as the Lord had spoken to him.* (Genesis 12:4)

Abram did just what <u>his God</u> told him to do. The writer of the New Testament book of Hebrews, penned many years later, identifies this man as a man of faith.[73] He believed God and then acted on his belief. This belief, Abram's trust in God was so pleasing to Him.[74] It was by this trust, this faith, that the relationship between Abram and God was formed.

Like all relationships involving humans, there were rocky times because of that forever-present bent toward sin. Yet, over the years, over the many travels, steps and missteps of Abram, this God remained faithful. He protected His carrier of the righteous seed, and Abram's beloved, Sarai. As the years passed, their relationship grew ever closer. God changed

---

[73] *"By faith Abraham, when he was called, obeyed by going out to a place which he was to receive for an inheritance; and he left, not knowing where he was going. ⁹ By faith he lived as a stranger in the land of promise, as in a foreign land, living in tents with Isaac and Jacob, fellow heirs of the same promise; ¹⁰ for he was looking for the city which has foundations, whose architect and builder is God"* (Hebrews 12:8-10).

[74] *"And without faith it is impossible to please Him, for the one who comes to God must believe that He exists, and that He proves to be One who rewards those who seek Him"* (Hebrews 11:6).

Abram's name to Abraham (The Father of Many Nations) and Sarai's name to Sarah (Princess). He also made more promises to Abraham, including granting him a vast area of land and innumerable offspring. God even made a blood covenant with Abraham to guarantee that all the promises would be fulfilled. Yet, no offspring came forth from Sarah. The clock was ticking. How could he be the father of many nations without an heir?

Where was Satan when all this was going on between God and Abraham? He was there, just waiting for the big opportunity. The next phase of the Seed-Kill Campaign was about to get underway.

As Abraham and Sarah both reached old age, they began to question how they would fulfill God's promises. Sarah was still barren and Abraham's ability to father a child—an heir—soon became doubtful. If they were ever to become parents, now was the time.

In a move that could only have been inspired by Satan, the aged couple developed a fallback plan—a plan that would have a disastrous effect on the world for ages to come. It was Sarah's idea to continue the righteous line by using her handmaiden as a surrogate mother.[75] Abraham, while he could still father a child, would impregnate Hagar, Sarah's Egyptian slave woman, as the carrier of the future of Abraham's race. This child would be the heir that God promised. Through him, Abraham would be the father of many nations and the carrier of the seed through which all the peoples of the world would be blessed. That's what God promised, and that's what the four of them (Abraham, Sarah, Hagar, and Satan) would deliver.

---

[75] This approach to continuing the lineage of the father was an accepted practice in the culture of Abram's day.

And so it happened as they planned: once again, a son of God came into a daughter of men. Sound familiar? Think back to the Nephilim—except this time, the son of God wasn't an unrighteous angel. The son of God in this case was the declared-righteous Abraham, the father of the Jewish race, the carrier of the righteous seed. And this time, the daughter of men happened to be of the lineage of the Gentiles, an Egyptian, a slave. Abraham and Sarah were chosen by God as progenitors of the Rescuer. Hagar was not.

Satan was riding high. The mixing of spirit with flesh would produce a wonderful imposter. Nine months later, it did. The firstborn of Abraham was Ishmael, the inheritor, the carrier of Abraham's seed. Satan did it. He blunted the righteous line. Ishmael was the byproduct of a prince and a slave, a Jew and a Gentile becoming *one flesh*. Ishmael was a tainted offspring. There would be no great Rescuer that would crush Satan's head coming from Ishmael's tainted line. The mixing of the righteous with the unrighteous can only produce the unrighteous.[76]

Victory at last! It took a while, but the Seed-Kill Campaign worked. Satan tasted victory, but he didn't savor it that whole first year after Ishmael's birth. Satan kept his guard up while trying to anticipate a response from God that never came. From the second through the fifth year of the child's growth, Satan became increasingly relaxed. Abraham loved his boy, Ishmael. As Abraham grew more attached to his son, Satan grew more confident of his success. When Ishmael turned ten, Satan finally chalked it

---

[76] The apostle Paul, in addressing the immoral behavior of the Corinthian believers, reminds them of this very concept. He reminds them that by participating in sexual relations with prostitutes, they are becoming "one flesh" with them, which is a mixture that is unreconcilable. *"Do you not know that your bodies are parts of Christ? Shall I then take away the parts of Christ and make them parts of a prostitute? [a]Far from it! 16 Or do you not know that the one who joins himself to a prostitute is one body with her?"* (1 Corinthians 6:15-16).

up as a complete win against God and man. He would keep his position as "Ruler of This World."[77]

When Ishmael turned thirteen,[78] God finally responded to Satan's deceptive plan by appearing to Abraham, instructing him that his wife Sarah would have a child and it would be through this child to come that the covenant with Abraham would be fulfilled. But Abraham was disappointed. He loved his boy, Ishmael, and pleaded with God to accept him as the covenant child, which, of course, God denied.[79] However, because of God's love for Abraham, God assured him that his son Ishmael would be greatly blessed.[80]

A year later, Ishmael, now on the brink of manhood, saw his competition being born. Ishmael was still the firstborn, though, and to him would go all the rights of the oldest son. He would get a double share of Abraham's wealth and status. It was only natural. But Ishmael and Hagar found that the natural order of things was not to be followed by Abraham. God had commanded that it was through the offspring of Sarah, her son Isaac,

---

[77] Jesus identified Satan by the title of "Ruler of This World." *"Now judgment is upon this world; now* **the ruler of this world** *will be cast out. 32 And I, if I am lifted up from the earth, will draw all people to Myself"* (John 13:31-32).

[78] Abraham was 86 when Ishmael was born, and 100 when Isaac was born. God visited Abraham when he was 99, the year before Isaac's birth.

[79] God could not and would not accept Ishmael because he did not carry the seed of the Rescuer. Ishmael was the son of the slave girl—a picture of bondage. Isaac, the son of a princess was a picture of royalty. He was to be the prototype of the coming Rescuer by being offered as a sacrifice—one that would be accepted. Ishmael could never be the prototype of the Rescuer. In fact, any sacrifice offered to God by Abraham involving Ishmael would be rejected.

[80] See Genesis 17:20 for God's promise to Abraham regarding Isaac.

that the covenant would be continued. All rights of the firstborn would pass to the firstborn of the princess, not the slave.

After another year or so, when Isaac was weaned from his mom and a big celebration was given, Sarah noticed something about Ishmael that put her on guard.

> *Now Sarah saw the son of Hagar the Egyptian, whom she had borne to Abraham, mocking Isaac.* (Genesis 21:9)

The eyes of a mom don't miss much around her child—particularly her firstborn son. Sarah saw the young man's demeanor around her little child, and from her response, she likely feared for Isaac's life. She was concerned that either Ishmael or Hagar, his mother, posed a threat to Isaac as they sought to protect their inheritance. Sarah's response was to demand that Hagar and her son be driven from the camp and all connection with the inheritance from Abraham be cut off. When Abraham petitioned God, He confirmed Sarah's demand and told him that all his descendants would come forth from Isaac.

The impostor and his mother were driven from the camp as God had commanded. From this point forward, God saw Isaac, and only Isaac, as the son of Abraham! Spiritually, Abraham had only one son who would continue the righteous line that would carry the seed of the woman and one day crush the head of Satan.

But don't think that Satan's deception was a total failure. Much of the chaos that has plagued the Middle East through the centuries, and continues to this day, can be traced back to the birth of the child to the slave woman.

Chapter 10

———··◁∞▷··———

The Seed-Kill Campaign

Genocide

"Civil Wars happen when the victimized are armed. Genocide happens when they are not."—A.E. Samaan

The aroma from the Vietnamese restaurant emanates from the far side of the building, where there is a bakery. Dong Phuong, located on the periphery of New Orleans where Asian refugees settled in the early '70s, became a popular eatery for folks travelling through Chalmette, Louisiana. As good as the soups and entrees are, it is the smells from the bakery attached to the restaurant that light up the senses. The pastries rival any in New Orleans.

New Orleans cooking has had many influences, and the French were one of the European imports that have made a huge impact. The French were among the first settlers of the city, even before America was born. As strong an impact as they've had on our country, the French have had an even bigger impact on the Vietnamese. This small country in Indochina was defeated by the French in 1862 and became part of the French Empire. Full French colonization began in 1897. As a servant state under French rule, Western capitalists moved in to acquire land and establish rubber plantations for export. With the French "masters" came their cooks, recipes, and ingredients. The Vietnamese people adapted to these new bosses and learned to prepare French food and pastries that rivaled European cuisine in France.

During the Second World War, the Japanese temporarily drove the French out of Indochina and Vietnam. At the end of the war, when the French returned to reestablish control, the Vietnamese sought independence. They organized to throw off the yoke of French colonialism. A communist organization known as the Viet Minh was formed as a national liberation movement in Vietnam, while all the countries in Indochina under French dominance (Laos, Cambodia, and Vietnam) rebelled in the French Indochina War.

> *Like shooting fish in a barrel.*—Viet Minh *Soldier after the Battle of Dien Bien Phu*

The Indochina War in Vietnam eventually culminated in victory at the Battle of Dien Bien Phu. The city of Dien Bien Phu is in a remote location in the northwest corner of Vietnam. During the Indochina War with the French, the Viet Minh used this city as a financial source for its operations since it was known for trafficking high volumes of opium. The French had created a heavily fortified base deep in a valley outside the city to monitor and block the opium trade. Dien Bien Phu became a critical chess piece. If the French could maintain control of the base, it would severely reduce the finances needed to continue funding the Viet Minh's insurrection. If the Viet Minh could destroy the French, it would demonstrate that France could no longer control this Asian country.

The Viet Minh strategy was to surround and lay siege to the base and force the French to surrender. Because they were surrounded and all inroads were cut off, the only means for the French to continue fighting in this remote stronghold of theirs was continual resupply of fresh troops and supplies by air. An airstrip on the base gave the French air force access for its planes to land. To put an end to this capability, the Viet Minh, through sheer human willpower, moved artillery pieces up the steep mountain that overlooked the French base. Once these batteries were in place, it was only a matter of time.

Firing "downhill," the Viet Minh easily lobbed ordinance onto the French. The French tried to respond with their own cannon fire to eliminate the Viet Minh's batteries, but artillery fire uphill caused the trajectory of the French rounds to fall well short of the Vietnamese cannons. Like the Viet Minh soldier said, "When you have surrounded your enemy and have fire superiority from a higher point, it is like shooting fish in a barrel!" On May 7, 1954, the French-held garrison at Dien Bien Phu in Vietnam fell after a four-month siege led by Vietnamese nationalist Ho Chi Minh. After the fall of Dien Bien Phu, the French pulled out of the country in defeat.[81]

That must have been what Satan thought for his next battle against God and Abraham's descendants: "I've got them surrounded in one place. It will be easy to wipe out this entire lineage and put an end to God's plan to remove me – to crush my headship of the earth. It will be like shooting fish in a barrel!"

How did the people of Abraham get themselves into such a predicament that their entire race could be so easily eliminated from the earth?

The righteous line that carried the seed of the woman was through Abraham and then through Isaac's son, Jacob. God

---

[81] *Dien Bien Phu & the Fall of French Indochina, 1954*. Office of the Historian, US Department of State. Retrieved May 12, 2024, from https://history.state.gov/milestones/1953-1960/dien-bien-phu#:~:text=In%20early%201954%2C%20the%20French,links%20on%20the%20Laotian%20border.

had maintained and confirmed the covenant and guarantees He made with Abraham, Isaac, and Jacob. Jacob, whose name God had changed to Israel, had twelve sons. Each of the sons would become the head of a tribe, and the people of the tribes together became known by Jacob's new name, Israel. They were the people of Israel, the twelve tribes of Israel! These tribes settled in the land God led Abraham to— the land of Canaan. However, these people were not settled in the sense that they built houses and cities. They were nomads. They stayed in tents and moved to where the land would support them.

Through a series of sinful misadventures (too numerous to cover here), all these nomadic people packed up their tents and the few belongings they had and followed the food trail to Egypt when food became scarce. There was a severe famine in their land. So, the entire flock of the twelve tribes of Israel moved into Egypt seeking food.

God had divinely provided food for all of Jacob's (Israel's) tribes. Jacob and all the people were welcomed into the land by the Egyptians, again, due to the work and foreknowledge of God placing Joseph, the eleventh son of Jacob, in a critical high position in the Egyptian government.[82]

Thanks to the planning and management of the young Hebrew, Joseph, Egypt had prepared for this intense famine. The Egyptians had food, and if they had food and welcomed the people, there was no reason for the tribes of Israel to

---

[82] The reader is encouraged to check out the entire story of God's providence for the people of Israel through the eleventh son of Jacob – a boy named Joseph who was sold into slavery by his brothers, taken to Egypt where he was thrown into prison, yet eventually became the right hand of the Pharoah. Genesis chapters 37 through 46 cover this amazing work of God through this faithful young man.

leave. Time passed, and over the years, Joseph and the other eleven sons of Jacob died. Although the original tribal leaders were gone, the people of Israel grew larger and stronger. In fact, the population of the tribes of Israel grew at such a rate that it raised alarm among the Egyptians.

The people of Israel stayed too long. Scripture doesn't reveal at what point the Israelites started to become servants to the Egyptians, to the point of becoming slaves. What we do know is that when Joseph, Israel's primary influencer in the Egyptian government died, he was quickly forgotten, and the people of Israel rapidly fell from favor.

> *Now a new king arose over Egypt, who did not know Joseph.* (Exodus 1:8)

All of what this Hebrew by the name of Joseph had done for Egypt as the right hand of the then-Pharaoh was old history. There was a new sheriff in town! When he assumed command, this new Pharaoh only associated a Hebrew as a slave of Egypt—totally under his control.

This was Satan's opening. It would be like shooting fish in a barrel. Every person linked genetically to Abraham was corralled in one place and they were under the control of the Egyptians—who were under Satan's control! These Egyptians were great idolaters. Horus, the sun god, Osiris, the goddess of fertility, Anubis, the god of the underworld, and other deities of Satan were worshipped by the people of Egypt. The use of powerful magic by the diviners of courts was a common practice.[83]

---

[83] That the Egyptians were controlled and supported by Satan and his demons is evident from this passage in Exodus 7:11-12: *"Then Pharaoh also called for the **wise men** and the **sorcerers**, and they too, the **soothsayer priests** of Egypt, did the same with their **secret arts**. For each one threw down his staff, and they turned into serpents."*

This new "king" Pharaoh was a direct tool of Satan. This Pharaoh, thought by many historians to be Ramses II,[84] was a type of antichrist, just like his ancient predecessor by the name of Nimrod. The yet future end-time battles that will occur during a horrific time on Earth known as the Tribulation, will involve the real antichrist. He will operate with supernaturally influenced powers and be supported by an army of demons to carry out Satan's wishes, just like this Pharaoh. Because idolatry involves demon worship,[85] Pharaoh, whose land is filled with idols, is a picture of the future antichrist.

This new Pharaoh will be Satan's man to once-and-for-all put an end to the Abrahamic line, which will kill the seed God said would crush Satan's head. He will conduct his own holocaust and methodically wipe out this people group known as Israel. Genocide is one of Satan's methods that will be seen in future battles. For the antichrist-type Pharaoh, it is the method of choice.

Conducting mass slaughter of the Hebrews would negatively impact the production capabilities these hard-working slaves delivered to Egypt. Satan had to be patient and use time to his advantage. It took some thinking, but when he hit on the solution, Pharaoh saw that it was foolproof. His plan was simple, efficient, and brilliant. He would methodically wipe out these people of the sons of Israel over a short generation of time.

---

[84] *Moses and Pharoah*. Brittanica. Retrieved May 12, 2024, from https://www.britannica.com/biography/Moses-Hebrew-prophet/Moses-and-Pharaoh

[85] The Apostle, Paul, when writing to the Corinthians, warned them about being associated in any way with idolatry, because demonology and idolatry go hand-in-hand. *"But I say that things which the Gentiles sacrifice, they sacrifice to demons and not to God; and I do not want you to become partners with demons"* 1 Corinthians 10:20).

*Then the king of Egypt spoke to the Hebrew mid-
wives, one of whom was named Shiphrah, and the
other was named Puah; ¹⁶ and he said, "When you
are helping the Hebrew women to give birth and
see them upon the birthstool, if it is a son, then you
shall put him to death; but if it is a daughter, then she
shall live."* (Exodus 1:15-16)

The plan was so effective and demonically brilliant that it
could come from only one source. After all, who could think
of such a horrific concept? Within 13-15 years, there would
be no male Hebrew children to have union with Hebrew
women. The women of child-bearing age would be mated
with slaves of different races, with the resulting offspring
being of mixed heritage and members of a non-homogene-
ous group, rather than one that maintained strict control of
their culture, such as the children of Israel. Egypt's problem
would be solved, and more importantly, Satan's problem of
a seed of the woman that would crush his head would be
eliminated. Abraham's race would be terminated, and with
it, God's plan would be defeated. The Seed-Kill Campaign
would finally result in total victory.

After a few false starts in which the Hebrew midwives cir-
cumvented Pharaoh's command to kill the male children
when they were delivered, he then instructed his own people
to kill each Hebrew newborn male. They were to immediately toss the infant boy into the Nile.

Once again, it was time for the Most High to intercede.

God's hand guided a reed-covered basket placed in the river.
The basket contained an infant Hebrew boy. The divinely
guided basket was protected from the waters and crocodiles
of the Nile as it reached its destination at the dock of Pharaoh's daughter. The child would be raised under the nose of

Pharaoh until manhood. This Egyptian-raised Hebrew would be rejected by Pharaoh and driven into the desert to die. It would be at God's time when this man of Abraham's seed would return from the desert to carry God's message to Pharaoh, "Let My people go!"

The child's name was Moses.

Satan's war with God continues…

Chapter 11

―――――⚬∞⚬―――――

The Seed-Kill Campaign

The Battle of Elah Valley

"Giants are not what we think they are. The same qualities that appear to give them strength are often the sources of great weakness."—Malcolm Gladwell

It wasn't a fair fight! The Battle of Fada was little known to most people. This wasn't a big battle. On the international stage, one would say it was insignificant. It was fought by two third-world countries located on the other side of the world. Back in 1987, the battle barely made the evening news on most American and British television stations. It just wasn't worth the attention of the media.

This little battle might not have been important to the news media or even to the average person, but it caught the attention of generals throughout the world. American military strategists and tacticians studied this relatively small and generally insignificant conflict with great intensity. Video footage from the battle was included in every tactical lesson taught to American mobile armored commanders down to the individual tank crew. It was that important!

In a move to gain greater control of the oil supply in his region, Libyan dictator Muammar Gaddafi positioned his occupation troops near Fada, a city in the North African country of Chad. Gaddafi had invaded Chad, his southerly neighbor, in the hope of capturing and controlling the country while it was weakened from a recent civil war. The city of Fada is located well inside Chad's northeastern border, separating Chad and Libya. This was the second year of the war between the two countries. The Libyan occupation force that Gaddafi had positioned at Fada was formidable. It included 1,200 well-armed infantry supported by a large armored vehicle group consisting of over 100 Russian-made T-55 tanks and additional BMP-1 armored personnel carriers.

It was the Soviet T-55 tank that made Libya's defense so stout. The T-55 is an intimidating mass of mobile steel. An out-of-vision battle tank crashing through the woods as trees crumble before it and treetops disappear when the unseen monster moves toward its objective can be gut-wrenching. It is well described as a terror weapon. With 105 of these mechanized beasts, Libya was well armed for the coming Battle of Fada.

Chad approached the battle with a sizeable group of infantry to outnumber the Libyans. However, Chad's commanders had a problem: they had no tanks. What they did have was the knowledge that the Libyans were trained by the Russians in conventional warfare strategies and tactics, and they recognized the battle would be fought in the desert.

To counter the anticipated conventional tank attack by Libyan forces, the Chad commanders decided to create a very flexible weapon—a Toyota pickup truck armed with a French Milan anti-tank weapon mounted on the truck bed. There was one driver for the truck and one weapons man in the truck bed to aim and fire the anti-tank projectile.

A tank against a Toyota pickup truck? It just doesn't sound like a fair fight.

It wasn't.

After the battle was over, 92 of the 105 T-55 tanks had been destroyed, compared to only 3 Toyotas lost to the tanks. The Chadian victory was overwhelming. The slow-moving tanks had difficulty maneuvering in the sands of the desert, while the little, light, mobile Toyotas buzzed around the tanks, always maintaining a position ahead of the slowly rotating tank turrets and away from the tank's fixed-mounted machine guns. When the truck was in position, the anti-tank weapons man in the truck bed did his work very effectively.

From the opening bell, it just wasn't a fair fight.

Saul was king of Israel, head of twelve nomadic tribes that were making the transition from wandering herders to owners of the Promised Land with permanent settlements.

With Saul as their first king, the loosely organized nation of Israel continued its ongoing series of battles to defend the Promised Land that it occupied. All the nations surrounding these people of God were Gentiles, and most were potential enemies. Israel's arch-nemesis was the Philistines. They were pagans and worshippers of false deities that were offshoots of the idols Satan introduced in Babylon so many years prior.

These Philistines were a people who settled in five independent city-states (Ashkelon, Ashdod, Ekron, Gath, and Gaza) along the coastal plains of the Mediterranean, today known as the Gaza Strip. Although each city-state had its own king and was independent of the other city-states, the Philistines were unified and acted as one against a common enemy such as Israel.

Unlike the agriculturally based Israelite farmers, the Philistines were workers of iron. They were known for their superior military, advanced technology, and weaponry.

At the time of Saul and David, the Philistines were one of Israel's most important enemies. As a people, they were skilled at working with iron forged weapons, which gave them the ability to make impressive chariots. With these chariots of war, they dominated the coastal plains...[86]

At the Battle of Elah Valley, Saul and the Israelites were positioned on one mountain overseeing the valley, while the enemy forces of the Philistines were positioned on the opposite mountain. It appears that neither side was willing to launch the initial attack because doing so would be giving up the high ground and descending into the valley. Each side was waiting for the other to attack. It was during this time that a giant[87] by the name of Goliath came down from the Philistine high ground and shouted a champion challenge[88]

---

[86] Bible Affirming Truth. *DAVID AND GOLIATH*. One Page. Retrieved May 16, 2024, from https://www.onepagebiblesummary.com/bat/bat_05.php

[87] Goliath was from Gath, a Philistine city, but he wasn't a Philistine. He was a giant that likely descended from the line of Anak and took refuge with the Philistines when Israel invaded the mountain home of the giants of Anak.

"Thus they told him, and said, 'We went in to the land where you sent us; and it certainly does flow with milk and honey, and this is its fruit. [28] Nevertheless, the people who live in the land are strong, and the cities are fortified and very large; and moreover, we saw the descendants of Anak there'" (Numbers 13:27-28).

[88] It was common practice for two warring armies to pick a champion for a fight to the death. The winning (living) soldier, his king, and his army would be the victors of the battle. The losing king and his army would then surrender, thus saving countless lives on both sides.

"He stood and shouted to the ranks of Israel and said to them, "Why do you come out to draw up in battle array? Am I not the Philistine and you servants of Saul? Choose a man for yourselves and let him come

to the Israelite soldiers. Of course, facing a 9-foot soldier in hand-to-hand combat was overwhelming to the Israelite soldiers, and no champion of King Saul's was anxious to step forward to do battle.

This one battle between two men from opposing sides was critical. The outcome would determine the fate of the people of Israel. A loss would once again mean slavery for them. They would return to a position of submission under the will of people who were controlled by Satan. They would be slaves again, just as they were under Pharaoh's Egyptians. The servitude of the people of Israel to Satan's idolatrous Philistines would jeopardize the line that carried the seed of the woman – the seed that would one day give birth to the Rescuer – the One who would crush the head of Satan.

Satan's giant champion of the Philistines made continuous derogatory and challenging statements to Israel's king and his soldiers over a period of 40 days while the stalemate continued. His statements were ultimately meant as insults to Israel's God. As David said when he heard the taunts of Goliath, *"For who is this uncircumcised Philistine, that he should taunt the armies of the living God?"* (1 Samuel 17:26).

David had brought food from home for his three oldest brothers who were soldiers on the front lines. While there, he heard of the taunts from Goliath and expressed his disdain for the insults made to God. King Saul, upon hearing of David's replies of faith, sent for him and agreed to allow him to serve as his champion to fight Goliath.

---

down to me. [9] If he is able to fight with me and kill me, then we will become your servants; but if I prevail against him and kill him, then you shall become our servants and serve us" (1 Samuel 17:8-9).

From the opening bell, it wasn't a fair fight. Goliath was huge with oversized armor and heavy weaponry suited for conventional hand-to-hand combat in mass formation. In this arrangement, infantry troops were lined shoulder-to-shoulder for mass combat against the enemy's similarly positioned troops. In mass battle formation, foot movement and agility were of no benefit. Positioning a man of Goliath's size and strength on the front line would have made him a virtual killing machine. He only needed to destroy the man in front of him and plow through the mass of humanity with his enormous strength—one slow step at a time.

But in an open field in the valley of Elah, with only two combatants, the heavily armed, bulky giant was not just ineffective, he was an easy target. Satan's champion was a Soviet T-55 tank in the desert.

David took the opposite tactic by rejecting armor of any kind and refusing to carry heavy weaponry. He simply selected five smooth stones for his shepherd's sling—an accurate and deadly weapon in the hands of a properly trained marksman.[89] The dense stones carried sufficient knockdown weight, and the smooth surface facilitated accuracy over a longer distance. As a result, God's man was very mobile with a super-lightweight weapon that could be fired beyond the reach of a heavy spear thrown by a giant weighed down with armor. David could fire five rounds while the giant's single javelin would fall well short of David's position.

It was over almost as soon as the fight started. David came down from the mountain where the Israelite army stood,

---

[89] A Shepherd's Sling can generate stopping power equivalent to a magnum 44 pistol. See: https://www.nationalgeographic.com/history/article/ancient-slingshot-lethal-44-magnum-scotland

quickly moved toward the giant, and, staying beyond the spear-chucking distance of Satan's champion, launched his first and only missile. Goliath went down in a heap after being struck in the forehead. Then, using Goliath's own sword, David killed the beast.

With this victory, David became the hero of Israel and its favorite son. The women sang his praises in comparison to King Saul's accomplishments.

> *It happened as they were coming, when David returned from killing the Philistine, that the women came out of all the cities of Israel, singing and dancing, to meet King Saul, with tambourines, with joy and with musical instruments. [7] The women sang as they played, and said, "Saul has slain his thousands, And **David his ten thousands**." [8] Then Saul became very angry, for this saying displeased him; and he said, "They have ascribed to David ten thousands, but to me they have ascribed thousands. Now what more can he have but the kingdom?" [9] Saul looked at David with suspicion from that day on.* (1 Samuel 18:6-9)

How quickly Satan had recovered from the loss at the Valley of Elah! Pride had shown its ugly head again. The very ingredient in Satan's downfall had infected King Saul. His pride was damaged, and David was the cause of it. Satan was back in business.

David would become king, and Saul knew it. Try as he (and Satan) might to hunt down and kill David over the following years, God would not permit it. David was God's anointed to rule Israel upon Saul's death. Although Saul was king, he did not come from the royal line of Judah as David did. It was David's lineage that would carry the seed. It was from

David's offspring that a woman would have this royal seed, which would be the Rescuer to crush the head of Satan.

> *When your days are complete and you lie down with your fathers, I will raise up **your descendant** after you, who will **come forth from you**, and I will establish his kingdom. [13] He shall build a house for My name, and **I will establish the throne of his kingdom forever**.* (2 Samuel 7:12-14)

The attack failed to eliminate the royal carrier of the seed that will one day crush Satan's head. Throughout David's life, Satan went after him, and at times, with great success. David sinned, sometimes in the worst of ways. But God is faithful, and He keeps His promises. David remained on the throne until his death as an old man. Under David, the twelve tribes unified as one, and Israel became a nation to be feared. In their region, Israel was a superpower. The royal line continued through David to his son Solomon, the wisest of rulers, and then to the future carriers of the royal seed.

One day, the Rescuer will be born.

Until then, the Seed-Kill Campaign of Satan continues ...

Chapter 12

The Seed-Kill Campaign

Dragnet

"The facts ma'am, just the facts."—Sgt Joe Friday, LAPD

They had the facts. They should have known. All the necessary data were contained in documents at their disposal. They should have known He was coming. They didn't know the exact day and time, but they had all the information needed to bracket the time of His arrival. That would have gotten them close enough.

In the old war movies on television, there is often a soldier or Marine with a set of field glasses; standing next to him is a radio man. The guy with the field glasses is called an F-O or Forward Observer. He's the person who radios in a fire mission to an artillery battery located at a fire base some 5 to 15 miles away. The men operating the howitzers at the fire base can't see what they're shooting at, but the F-O can. His job is to bracket the target by calling in map coordinates to the firebase control center for the first shot, then adjusting each consecutive shot with instructions such as "left two hundred, drop one hundred." Once two consecutive shells bracket the target (one burst on one side and one on the other side) within 50 meters, he will then instruct the guns to "fire for effect," dropping shrapnel from all six cannons at once. Bracketing is a logical and effective tool for hitting the target. It gets you close enough!

The religious leaders of Israel had plenty of information to target the approximate time of the arrival of the Rescuer. Just that one passage in the scroll of Daniel would have been sufficient to get them close enough.

> *So you are to know and understand that from the issuing of a decree to restore and rebuild Jerusalem, until Messiah the Prince, there will be seven weeks and sixty-two weeks; it will be built again, with streets and moat, even in times of distress. [26] Then after the sixty-two weeks, the Messiah will be cut off and have nothing.* (Daniel 9:25)

Using Daniel's prophetic writing, after the command to rebuild the city of Jerusalem, a total of 69 "weeks" of years (69 x 7 years) is equivalent to 483 years. From this calculation, the Sanhedrin could have bracketed the calculated date and begun looking for the birth of their Messiah up to fifty years earlier. The religious rulers looking for their Messiah would certainly have set out dragnets to examine people, information, and indicators that would lead them to the One. Wise men would have done this.

In fact, wise men did do this. They were called the Magi. Daniel, the prophet of Israel who had attained such great significance while captive in Babylon and Medo-Persia (Parthia of their day, and Iran today), recorded his prophecies in their country. Daniel was considered one of the great advisors and wise men of his time by the Persians. No doubt the Persian Magi of Christ's time had studied Daniel's scrolls, as well as Balaam's prophecy indicating that a star would signal the coming King of Israel.[90] When these two ingredients were

---

[90] *"I see him, but not now; I look at him, but not near; **A star shall appear from Jacob, A scepter shall rise from Israel**, And shall smash the [s]forehead of Moab, And overcome all the sons of Sheth"* (Numbers 24:17).

combined, the Magi had all the information they needed to search for the Promised One.

What about Satan? He knows Scripture better than any intense Bible student or scholar. He knew the approximate time. It appears that his strategy was akin to what the Japanese did on Iwo Jima. General Tadamichi Kuribayashi, the Japanese commander on Iwo Jima, recognized that he could not defeat the Marines by attempting to prevent an amphibious landing. Instead, he allowed the landing to take place unopposed. When the Marines saturated the beaches with men and material, they became easy targets for his artillery and machine gun emplacements. The enemy was allowed to land without opposition, and then Kuribayashi's men raked the beaches with their deadly fire. They were like fish caught in a dragnet.[91]

Satan's plan was the same as General Kuribayashi's. Aggressively pursuing the righteous line of the unborn seed to kill it had been an unsuccessful campaign strategy. This time, he would let the child be born,[92] put out a dragnet to locate Him, and then put an end to the Rescuer before He could even begin His mission. Satan had the objective for this next battle, and he had just the General to carry out his strategy—a man by the name of Herod the Great!

---

[91] *Iwo Jima and Okinawa: Death at Japan's Doorstep*. National WWII Museum. Retrieved May 15, 2024, from https://www.nationalww2museum.org/war/articles/iwo-jima-and-okinawa-death-japans-doorstep

[92] It was the little village girl, Mary, who became pregnant without the seed of the man. It was from her (*seed-of-the-woman*) bloodline and from the Holy Spirit who *overshadowed* her that she conceived the Rescuer. See Matthew 1:20-25 and Luke 1:30-35

Herod was a man of Arab origin. He wasn't a Jew. His father Antipater was an Edomite who became a convert to Judaism. Antipater had great political connections with Rome. He knew Julius Caeser and became procurator of Judea by his appointment. It was Caeser who pronounced Roman citizenship upon the Antipater family. After Antipater's death, his son Herod became great friends with Caeser's right-hand man, Mark Antony, who made him tetrarch (regional governor) of Galilee. After the Parthian invasion of Jerusalem (the Parthians were enemies of Rome), which forced Herod to flee the city, the Roman senate appointed him king of Judea and provided him with military force so that he could return to lay claim and hold the title, "King of the Jews."

In addition to being a wily politician, Herod was considered "Great," primarily for his architectural and building prowess. He was a builder of fortresses, temples, and cities. Herod built the port city of Caesarea, which became the capital of Palestine. Both the Antonia and Masada fortresses were constructed under Herod's reign. But he was most admired for the massive rebuilding project of the second temple in Jerusalem, which he transformed into an opulent work of architecture from a somewhat spartan construction completed by the returning Jews from exile in Babylon some 500 years earlier.

> *His most grandiose creation was the* <u>Temple</u>, *which he wholly rebuilt. The great outer court, 35 acres (14 hectares) in extent, is still visible as Al-Ḥaram al-Sharīf.*[93]

All that engineering and architectural talent was good, but what Satan loved about Herod was that he was a paranoid

---

[93] *Herod King of Judea.* Brittanica. Retrieved May 6, 2024, from https://www.britannica.com/biography/Herod-king-of-Judaea

killer. He had murdered Marianne, the one wife he loved (He had eight wives.), along with her two sons, her grandfather, and her mother. He also murdered his firstborn son, Antipater. He would do anything to protect his position and viewed those in line for his throne as enemies. When the Magi rolled into town looking for the One born king of the Jews, it set Herod off.

> *When Herod the king heard this, he was troubled[94], and all Jerusalem with him.* (Matthew 2:3)

What shook the entire city was that an entourage of Parthians[95] had ridden into town looking for the King of the Jews.

It is obvious that Herod and the priesthood were oblivious to the birth of the Rescuer since they scrambled to find factual information regarding the prophetic birthplace. Herod asked for the exact time that the Magi first observed the star indicating the Messiah had been born. This fact would help determine the approximate age of the child, which may have been up to two years old.[96]

---

[94] Herod was shaken because they asked for the one, "born king of the Jews." Herod was an appointed king and not part of Hebrew lineage. The Magi were looking for the Messiah, which would have threatened Herod's position with the people and Rome.

[95] Rome was at war with the Parthians (Persians). Unlike what is shown in movies and written in books, the Persian Magi would not have traveled by themselves. Since the Magi were high-ranking officials they would most likely have traveled with an armed escort. Their sudden appearance may have caused the Roman garrison to be put on alert, and the city population to become concerned. The number of Magi that arrived in Jerusalem seeking the new king is not given in Scripture, but it likely was not three men traveling alone.

[96] *What Was the Star of Bethlehem?* Got Questions. Retrieved May 10, 2024, from https://www.gotquestions.org/star-of-Bethlehem.html

Just off the shores of the south Louisiana coastline, in shallow bays that pocket the deteriorating marshes and small islands opening into the Gulf of Mexico, the pogey boats arrive. The boats come from their massive mother ship located in slightly deeper water not far away. Like killer whales, the boats all work together setting out the dragnets in search of their prize: a tiny bait fish called a "pogey" that will be crushed and mashed into a meal-like substance to be sold to petfood canners. The pogey boats rape the coastline of anything living when they haul in their nets. Before departing, the destroyers cull out of their nets the unwanted residue of their kill. Recreational fishermen weep at the stinking corpses of beautiful, speckled trout, redfish, and other game fish left floating with gaping mouths open—all caught in the dragnet of the killer pogey boats.

With Bethlehem as the location of his target identified and with the approximate age of the child, around two, Herod had all the information he needed. After the Magi bypassed Jerusalem on their return trip to Persia, Herod and Satan launched their brutal assault on the sleepy, little Bethlehem community. One has to wonder what it takes for a man to order the execution of these babies. But with Satan's hatred of mankind, it isn't hard to imagine. All little boys, two years and under, must be killed. The evil dragnet of Herod will trawl for the innocent just to protect his kingdom for a few years. And, for Satan, the dragnet will capture his prize. This Rescuer that God had sent to crush Satan's head won't make it to his third birthday.

But, the omniscient God, fully anticipating the danger to His Son, removed Him from the snare of Satan.

Now when they (the Magi) had gone, behold, an angel of the Lord appeared to Joseph in a dream and said, "Get up! Take the Child and His mother and flee to Egypt and stay there until I tell you; for Herod is going to search for the Child to kill Him." [14] So Joseph got up and took the Child and His mother while it was still night and left for Egypt. [15] He stayed there until the death of Herod; this happened so that what had been spoken by the Lord through the prophet would be fulfilled: "Out of Egypt I called My Son." (Matthew 2:13-15)

Herod's residue of bloodied streets, lifeless infants and toddlers, and screaming mothers were of no concern to Satan. His Seed-Kill Campaign had failed. The Rescuer had arrived and was alive and well.

A new strategy will be developed to deal with Satan's enemy #1.

Chapter 13

―――――•◦∞◦•―――――

The Impeccable Battle

"A woman is like a tea bag—you can't tell how strong she is until you put her in hot water."—Eleanor Roosevelt Seagraves

The pressure is on. It is qualification day. There are fifty locations with a number next to each location, all parallel to one another. Number 1 starts on the left, and it ends at Number 50 on the far right. The gunnery sergeant, with an intimidating command voice, is in the tower with a blaring loudspeaker at hand. At each location, a rifleman lies in a worn spot in the grass, a result of shooter after shooter, Marine after Marine, quickly assuming the prone firing position. Downrange, all the shooter sees is a low berm with an impact area behind it. The 1st Platoon riflemen of Alpha Company are positioned at their assigned numbers. With all fifty positions filled, fifty targets suddenly appear at the command from the tower.

Within seconds, the first crack of M-16 rifle fire is heard, followed by increasing cracks as each shooter zeroes in on his target. Every shot fired by every shooter is recorded. At the end of the day, each shooter's score is totaled. He must qualify. Every Marine must qualify as a rifleman. Every Marine, whether enlisted, NCO, or Officer, is first and foremost a rifleman. A tank officer is a rifleman. An artillery F-O is a rifleman. Even a chopper pilot or fighter pilot is a rifleman. Everyone must qualify to accomplish the mission.

Qualification. Validation. Under pressure.

The Rescuer, the Son of God, also had to qualify—not as a rifleman, but as the Rescuer. His attributes and character had to be tested and proven. But unlike riflemen who may qualify as experts, sharpshooters, or even marksmen with less than perfect scores, the Rescuer's qualifications had to be impeccable—without fault, a perfect score. He had to be tried, stretched, heated, and pressed. It was the only way to determine the certainty of his qualifications.

> *Then Jesus was led up by the Spirit into the wilderness to be tempted by the devil.* (Matthew 4:1)

It was the Holy Spirit who initiated these tests. It was God who demanded that His Son undergo the gauntlet. It was the Holy Spirit who took the Rescuer to this wilderness area, a severe location that is literally known as "The Devastation." This place is lonely, barren, and hard. It was just the environment needed to stress the candidate to His full capacity. Why the severe test? Because the Rescuer is a man, and it must be known by all mankind that He can be trusted, that He is dependable, and that He will not fail when men and women cry out His name in desperation for rescue.

The testing was critical to the Rescuer's mission. His mission was to crush the head of the serpent and thereby fulfill God's promise to the world. For the mission to be accomplished, the impeccability of the Rescuer was the key ingredient—one that could only be validated through testing. If any imperfection, no matter how slight, could be revealed in the testing process, the Rescuer would be disqualified, and Satan could retain the position he usurped from Adam so many years earlier.

The tester was hand-picked by God—he was none other than the Tempter—Satan, the one whose mission was to destroy the Rescuer. Satan, through the ages, had attempted to destroy the line carrying the seed of the woman, but he was defeated by God at every turn. His new strategy was to kill the Rescuer now that the "woman who knew no man"[97] had given birth to this *Rescuer* some thirty years earlier. But now, the job would be much easier. He didn't need to kill this man after all. Satan needed to cause just one failure in this testing—just one—and the battle was won, the war was over.

The Tempter-Tester knew the Son as a Spirit. Lucifer had worshipped the Son in the third heaven when he served as God's seraphim. But now, the Son was flesh—a man. The Rescuer was a strange combination of human flesh and divine Spirit, something foreign to Satan. It appeared as if He was something of a *hybrid human.*[98] How could this combination be? How much was human and how much was deity? What did the Son in heaven have to give up to become a human on Earth? What part of Him was now vulnerable?

In considering these questions, Satan developed a plan of attack. He would assault the weakest part of this Rescuer—the human part. After all, Satan had a perfect record when attacking and causing human failure. He got Eve by tricking

---

[97] Mary's Son, conceived by the Holy Spirit, the Son of God. See Matthew 1:20-25 and Luke 1:30-35

[98] The term "hybrid" is one that the author has used, indicating that Satan may not have fully understood the dual nature (full deity and full humanity) of the Rescuer. Only God knows Satan's mind and thought processes. Had Satan understood that the Rescuer was fully God, what would have been his motivation to conduct the temptation, knowing that God is impeccable?

her. Then he got Adam. With the same basic approach, he got every human offspring since Adam.

For the upcoming battle, the stage was perfectly set for Satan. Forty days. Now that number (40) sounds just like something God had arranged. Forty is a significant number in God's Word. It is comprehensive. Moses spent forty years in the wilderness as a shepherd before God called him to lead His people out of Egypt. The flood covered the earth for forty days. The Hebrews were punished with wandering in the wilderness for forty years until their generation died. And now, the Rescuer would be forty long days in the same wilderness without food.[99]

The first of the final two temptations was for the Rescuer to prove His relationship with the Father. Each temptation begins with, "If you are the Son of God."

The first temptation involved hunger. God doesn't need to eat, but man does. The humanity of the Rescuer was zeroed in on by the Tempter. He wasn't just hungry; He was significantly weakened from lack of food. The wily Tempter suggested that the Rescuer could recover from His extreme condition by merely accessing His deific abilities and converting stones into loaves of bread. In doing so, the Rescuer would have validated His deity while nourishing His humanity. Both "parts" of Him would benefit.

What the Tempter knew was that by following his suggestion, the Rescuer would no longer be in submission to the will of the Father for food and would therefore violate the very standard that He was being tested on. It was God's will

---

[99] There is no detailed record of what happened during the forty days leading up to the final 3-part temptation, but Luke 4:1-2 states that the Rescuer was subject to temptation throughout the forty days.

for the Rescuer to be fully dependent on the Father and to be in complete submission to Him.[100] The Rescuer struck back in response to Satan's temptation by quoting Scripture[101]— by which He declared His trust in the Father and the Father's Word. His response ended the first round.

The second round involved Satan's challenge, which was supported by Scripture. If Scripture was the basis for the reasoning behind the Rescuer's response to the first challenge, then the Tempter could package his next offering with a beautiful quote from God's Word.[102] It all sounded so good!

The challenge went something like this: "If you really do totally trust in God, then throw yourself over this high cliff and prove what God's Word says. God will see what is happening and send angels to protect you from the fall. That is, if you really do trust in God." This temptation was again aimed at the human side of this humanoid. This time, Satan was targeting the Rescuer's pride. The act of the Rescuer throwing Himself off the temple high point (which was, of course, always packed with people) and having angels provide a soft

---

[100] Later, when faced with the most difficult test imaginable—one that He could easily escape by acting on His deity—the Rescuer would again be in total submission and say, "Not My will, but Thine be done" (Luke 22:42).

[101] *"But He answered and said, "It is written: 'Man shall not live on bread alone, but on every word that comes out of the mouth of God'"* (Matthew 4:4).

[102] In this passage, Satan demonstrated his ability to recall God's Word and then use it to attack his prey. *"Then the devil took Him along into the holy city and had Him stand on the pinnacle of the temple, and he said to Him, "If You are the Son of God, throw Yourself down; for it is written: 'He will give His angels orders concerning You'; and 'On their hands they will lift you up, so that You do not strike Your foot against a stone'"* (Matthew 4:5-6).

landing would be quite a demonstration to the people of how special this Rescuer was to God. The people would recognize His status as Rescuer, and then He could go on with His mission.

But the Rescuer recognized that by participating in this proposed act, He would be testing God to act against His will. It was God's will for the Rescuer to endure the full testing by keeping Himself fully dependent upon the Father. To literally bail out of the process would be to reject the test that the Holy Spirit led Him into while tempting the Father to send His angels as protection. The Rescuer rejected the sinful suggestion with Scripture that exposed the trap and declared that He would not test God.[103]

The final temptation had nothing to do with the Rescuer's Father-Son relationship with God. Satan went right to the totally human, sinful desire of lust—the lust of the eyes—the human desire to acquire, to grab all the world has to offer. After all, Satan had the power to deliver on this, since he is the god of this world. He put everything on the table for the Rescuer to see. He could have it all: wealth, possessions, pleasure, control—all without any pain or sacrifice from the Rescuer.

There was no trap in this one. It was raw! But, like the other temptations, this offer had one important "if," and the condition was plainly stated: the Rescuer had to fall down and worship Satan—just once—and the deal would be sealed.[104]

---

[103] *"Jesus said to him, "On the other hand, it is written: 'You shall not put the Lord your God to the test'"* (Matthew 4:7).

[104] *"Again, the devil *took Him along to a very high mountain and *showed Him all the kingdoms of the world and their glory; [9] and he said to Him, "All these things I will give You, if You fall down and [c]worship me"* (Matthew 4:8-9).

The Rescuer's response to serving this fallen angel over following His Father's will was quick and sure. In His response, the Rescuer's deity and authority were fully demonstrated with His final quotation of Scripture and the command for Satan to depart. The Tempter, defeated, had no choice but to leave Him.[105] Deity had spoken.

When the testing was over, Scripture proclaimed that the Rescuer was tested in every area that a human could be tempted with no resulting flaw, no failure, no sin—only sinless perfection.[106]

It appears that Satan viewed the Rescuer as a hybrid, a humanoid: half-deity and half-human. But the testing revealed someone quite different. It revealed One with a fully human nature, yet with the impeccability of the full nature of deity. There was no trade-off in this person. He gave up nothing of His deific nature to acquire a human nature,[107] and human

---

[105] *"Then Jesus *said to him, "Go away, Satan! For it is written: 'You shall worship the Lord your God, and [d]serve Him only.'"* Then the devil **left Him; and behold, angels came and began to serve Him"* (Matthew 4:10).

[106] *"For we do not have a high priest who cannot sympathize with our weaknesses, but One who has been tempted in all things just as we are, yet without sin"* (Hebrews 4:15).

[107] By taking on humanity, the Son left behind the glory and honor that was given to Him in heaven where He sat at the right hand of the Father. *"Have this attitude [e]in yourselves which was also in Christ Jesus, [6]who, as He already existed in the form of God, did not consider equality with God something to be [f]grasped, [7]but [g]emptied Himself by taking the form of a bond-servant and [h]being born in the likeness of men. [8]And being found in appearance as a man, He humbled Himself by becoming obedient to the point of death: death [i]on a cross"* (Philippians 2:5-8).

nature He acquired was not from Adam, but from the seed of the woman, His human mother. The testing revealed what theologians call the hypostatic *union.*[108] Our Rescuer is fully God and fully man.

God, as He sometimes does, had used Satan as His tool. It was the Tempter who was offered the opportunity to disqualify His Son. But while the Tempter failed in his mission to ruin the Son's credentials, he accomplished exactly what God had in mind: to reveal the perfection of His Son. In so doing, the Rescuer could go forth on His mission to crush the head of the serpent, Satan.

---

[108] The hypostatic union is the term used to describe how God the Son, Jesus Christ, took on a human nature, yet remained fully God at the same time. Jesus had always been God (John 8:58, 10:30), but at the incarnation, Jesus became a human being (John 1:14). The addition of the human nature to the divine nature is Jesus, the God-man. This is the hypostatic union, Jesus Christ, one Person, fully God and fully man.

Jesus' two natures, human and divine, are inseparable. Jesus will forever be the God-man, fully God and fully human, two distinct natures in one Person. Jesus' humanity and divinity are not mixed but are united without loss of separate identity. Jesus sometimes operated with the limitations of humanity (John 4:6, 19:28) and other times in the power of His deity (John 11:43; Matthew 14:18-21). In both, Jesus' actions were from His one Person. Jesus had two natures, but only one personality.
See: https://www.gotquestions.org/hypostatic-union.html

Chapter 14

<hr>

Eliminate the Rescuer

"When a Marine is wounded, surrounded, hungry, or low on ammo, he looks to the sky. He knows the choppers are coming."—Unknown

From the war in Vietnam and forward, the Medevac helicopter was seen by the ground troops as the Great Rescuer—the angel in the sky. The Medevac chopper pilots knew how critical their mission was: to get the wounded out of the battlefield and onto an operating table in record time. There is a concept called the golden hour, which wasn't formalized until the 1980s, but the principle was known to the corpsmen, the chopper pilots, and the infantrymen. It is the limit of time from being seriously wounded to being on the surgeon's operating table, after which the chances of survival start rapidly falling. Sixty minutes from battlefield to hospital was the golden hour of survival.

The pilots who flew these angels of care were known for their bravery. These were the Rescuers of their day because they sacrificially disregarded their own safety and the conditions around them as they dropped their machine into a "hot LZ"—a landing zone that was receiving enemy fire. Whatever it took, they were going to get their chopper in and get the wounded out. Everyone knew when that rescue vehicle arrived; it was clearly identified, and it was a welcome sight.

About two millennia ago, when the Rescuer arrived, it was a different story. He came right on time and was clearly identified, but the leaders of the people that He came to rescue outright rejected Him. In fact, they wanted to kill Him. That would be like the Marines shooting down their own Medevac chopper! But that's what the Rescuer faced—death at the hands of the people He was sent to rescue. What could possibly have been their motive to want to kill Him?

Satan would give them their motive. The god of this world had to stop the Rescuer from dying a pre-ordained death. The Most High God, the Son, and the Holy Spirit had developed the Rescue Plan for Humanity—even before the creation of the world on the first day.[109] That plan included a specific predestined process by which the Son would die. If the Rescuer lost His life by any other method, the mission would be a failure. Satan had to kill Him in whatever way he could, except by God's preordained method. Satan would use the leaders of the Jews, the Romans, and even the followers of the Rescuer to terminate the Son's mission.

The Rescuer had numerous confrontations with these leaders of the Jews. They were deeply religious, the so-called spiritual leaders of their people. One would think spiritual leaders would easily recognize the Spirit in the man who was fully God. But they did not and would not accept Him for who He was. It wasn't that they didn't have sufficient standards to measure Him by—they did. They had all of the Scriptures written by

---

[109] *"Blessed be the God and Father of our Lord Jesus Christ, who has blessed us with every spiritual blessing in the heavenly places in Christ, ⁴just as He chose us in Him **before the foundation of the world**, that we would be holy and blameless before Him"* (Ephesians 1:3-5).

their own prophets. They even had an amazing prophet in their day who clearly identified Him as the One to come.[110]

In addition to this forerunner prophet clearly identifying the man, the Rescuer performed the correct signs that Scripture claimed the One would deliver. In a confrontational conversation with these religious people, He declared:

> *If I do not do the works of My Father, do not believe Me; but if I do them, even though you do not believe Me, believe the works, so that you may know and understand that the Father is in Me, and I in the Father.* (John 10:37-38)

What works did He do that gave such testimony these spiritual leaders would have had to be blind to reject? Of His many supernatural works, there were two Messianic healing miracles[111] that were so extreme the religious leaders should have further investigated the Rescuer's claim as the Son of God:

- There was a man who had been blind from the moment he came from his mother's womb. The parents were embarrassed and looked down upon because of their baby's condition. The "great theologians" of their day taught that a person who was born blind or disfigured in some way was the result of the great sinfulness of the parents or of the child when he would become an adult.

---

[110] John the Baptist, the forerunner prophet was sent by God to identify the Rescuer. *"The next day he saw Jesus coming to him, and said, "Behold, the Lamb of God who takes away the sin of the world!"* (John 1:29).

[111] These healings were prophetic fulfillment of the promised Messiah of Israel.

The Rescuer healed this man born blind—something that had never been done **by anyone before**. When the man with the healed vision was being interrogated by the religious leaders, he identified the Rescuer as the One who performed the healing. When the leaders declared that the Rescuer was a sinner, the man responded, *"Since the beginning of time it has <u>never been heard</u> that anyone opened the eyes of a person born blind. 33 If this man were not from God, He could do nothing." 34 They answered him, "You were born entirely in sins, and yet you are teaching us?" So they put him out"* (John 9:32-34).

> ▪ Leprosy was an incurable disease in their day. There were no medications to cure it or to retard its growth and render it non-infectious. It was a disfiguring malady that was feared among the population to the extent that those who had it were considered unclean and forced to live in remote areas until they died. Being cleansed of this disease would have been viewed as a supernatural act of God.

When a man with the disease came to the Rescuer and asked for healing, He responded with a command, *"Be cleansed. As soon as He had spoken, immediately, the leprosy left him, and he was cleansed"* (See Mark 1:40-45).

The fact is that the religious leaders were spiritually blind[112] and had leprosy of the heart. They were part of Satan's cadre to eliminate the Rescuer. In a major confrontation with these leaders, the Rescuer said: *"You are **of your father the devil**, and **you want to do the desires of your father**. He was a murderer from the beginning"* (John 8:44).

---

[112] *"And even if our gospel is veiled, it is veiled to those who are perishing, in whose case **the god of this world has blinded the minds of the unbelieving** so that they will not see the light of the gospel of the glory of Christ, who is the image of God"* (2 Corinthians 4:3-4).

In this head-to-head battle, the Rescuer clearly defined these facts:

1. Satan (the Devil) was their "father," in the sense that they were of his spiritual seed, and was the exact opposite of the Rescuer, who is of the seed of His Father, God. Hence, it was only natural that these leaders, the seed of Satan, wanted to kill the Rescuer.

2. Because the spiritual leaders were of Satan's evil, spiritual heritage, they only obeyed him and opposed God and His Son.

3. Satan is a murderer, and he desires that his offspring also commit murder. The underlying implication is that he wanted these religious children of his to murder the Rescuer.

Their mission was clear. Satan, the murderer from the beginning, was orchestrating these blind hypocrites in the same way he manipulated Cain to murder Abel. Satan's pure hatred of God included the Rescuer because He is the Son of God, sent from the Father to carry out the rescue mission.

So many times, hatred boiled over to the point that these people of Satan rose up and attempted to kill the Rescuer. There was such a rage of hatred toward this man. They would either immediately try to lay hands on Him to kill Him or withdraw to methodically plot His demise. In one instance of raging venom, a religious denomination known as the Pharisees tried to kill Him because He challenged their practice of extending and modifying the Law of God into a religious tradition. This tradition was then used to burden the people, which was the exact opposite of the intent of the Law. This denomination made all types of rules centered around the Sabbath Day, which was specified by the Law of God as a day of rest for God's people. This simple law was expanded into rules and regulations vigorously enforced by priests and religious lawyers in their righteous robes. When the Rescuer performed a sign of His Sonship on the Sabbath, violating their tradition-law, they were furious and condemned His actions. When He proceeded to heal a man with a crippled hand on the Sabbath to demonstrate to them His power over their traditions, *"the Pharisees went out and conspired against Him, as to seeking how they might destroy Him"* (Matthew 12:1-14).

When the Rescuer visited His hometown of Nazareth, He was invited to read the Scripture of the Day in their synagogue. That Scripture prophesied about the coming Rescuer. After reading it, He told those listening that the person described in the prophecy was Him.

> *When the people in the synagogue heard this, they were very angry.* ²⁹*They got up and forced Jesus to go out of town. Their town was built on a hill. They took Jesus to the edge of the hill to throw him off.* ³⁰ *But he walked through the middle of the crowd and went away.* (Luke 4:28-30)

On two separate occasions, the Jews tried to stone Him to death. On both occasions, the Rescuer asserted His equality with His Father. The first was when He declared to them, "I and the Father are One!" In addition to His declaration, He reminded the people with stones in their hands that His works and miracles were from the Father, which supported His statement of equality. They then sought to arrest Him, but He *"eluded their grasp"* (John 10:39).

The second occasion involved a confrontation with the Jews regarding their claim to be children of Abraham. Jesus responded by stating that Abraham rejoiced to know that a Rescuer would be sent, which implied that He knew Abraham, personally. With that statement, the Jews ridiculed Him because Abraham had lived many centuries before and there was no way that this 32-

year-old man would have known him. His response caused them to pick up stones, *"Before Abraham was, I AM!"* This declaration infuriated them because the term, *"I AM,"* is one that is used only by God. *"Therefore they picked up stones to throw at Him, but Jesus hid Himself and left the temple grounds"* (John 8:59).

Why would such blinding hatred cause them to stone this man instead of fully investigating His claims? It was Satan who gave these evil men the motive to kill the Rescuer who came to crush the head of mankind's nemesis. The Devil planted fear in their minds of the threat this person posed to their religious system, organizations, and individual positions of power. This motive was never more evident than after Lazarus, a friend of the Rescuer, had died, and the Son of God raised his friend after being dead and buried for four days. That he was "very" dead was evident from one of Lazarus' sisters who warned the Rescuer not to go near the grave because of the stench of decay of his body.[113]

After this event, during which many people believed in the Rescuer, the religious leaders—the chief priests and members of the ruling Sanhedrin council—met to discuss this validating sign, as well as other signs He performed that were reported to them. They were worried, fearing they would lose their positions of control.

> *Therefore the chief priests and the Pharisees convened a council meeting, and they were saying, "What are we doing in regard to the fact that this man is performing many signs? If we let Him go on like this, all the people will believe in Him, and the Romans will come and*

---

[113] *"Jesus said, 'Remove the stone.' Martha, the sister of the deceased, said to Him, 'Lord, by this time there will be a stench, for he has been dead four days'"* (John 11:39).

take over both our place and our nation." (John 11:47-48)

Caiaphas, the high priest, quickly concluded that it would be advantageous for everyone to kill this person who kept performing validating signs that he was the Son of God, the promised Rescuer. For that reason, according to one of Satan's boys, He must die. After all, it was the expedient thing to do. From that meeting, they started plotting to kill Him.[114] But no matter how and for what reason they tried to kill the Rescuer, God would not allow Him to be taken. In every event where these Satan-inspired religious people sought to kill Him, He somehow escaped—He would not be captured or killed. He would not be stoned. He would not be thrown off a cliff. He would not be stabbed. He would not be beheaded. Try as he might, Satan could not orchestrate the preliminary death of God's Son by any method other than the one stated by God, which Satan was all too familiar with.

> *And I will make enemies of you and the woman, And of your seed and her Seed; He shall crush you on the head, And you shall bruise Him on the heel.* (Genesis 3:14)

There was only one God-approved form of execution that was acceptable because the murder of His Son had to be accomplished according to God's plan. It was this form of execution of the Rescuer, planned before time began, that would deliver a mortal wound to Satan.

Satan's head will be crushed.

The Rescuer's heel **must** be bruised. It was the heel that identified the kind of death the Son of God must endure.

---

[114] *"So from that day on they planned together to kill Him"* (John 11:53).

Chapter 15

---———⋅⋅◦∞◦⋅⋅———

Crushing the Head of the Serpent

"You will bruise his heel, but he will crush your head."—
God speaking to the serpent in the garden (Genesis 3:14)

Passover is a celebration designed to recall the Israelites' captivity as slaves to Pharaoh thirteen centuries before this date. Moses was sent to Pharaoh on numerous occasions to demand that he set God's people free. Each rejected demand was followed by a plague, after which Moses returned with the same demand from God. Finally, to force Pharaoh to release the Hebrews, God instructed Moses to deliver this message to the ruler of Egypt:

> *About midnight I am going out into the midst of Egypt, and all the firstborn in the land of Egypt shall die, from the firstborn of the Pharaoh who sits on his throne, to the firstborn of the slave girl who is behind the millstones; all the firstborn of the cattle as well.*
> (Exodus 11:4-5)

This was a deadly event that would kill the firstborn from every family—every family in the land of Egypt, including the Hebrews. To protect the Hebrews from His wrath, God instructed Moses that each household was to select a lamb—and examine that special lamb for fourteen days to ensure that it was spotless, without any defect. On the eve of the Passover, the lamb was to be killed (sacrificed) and some of its blood was to be put on the two vertical posts of the doorway to the family's house and on the overhead horizontal post of the doorway. When God descended upon Egypt that night to kill the firstborn, He would *pass over* any household that was marked with **the blood of the lamb.**

**Blood on the Lentil
(overhead beam)
and the doorposts**

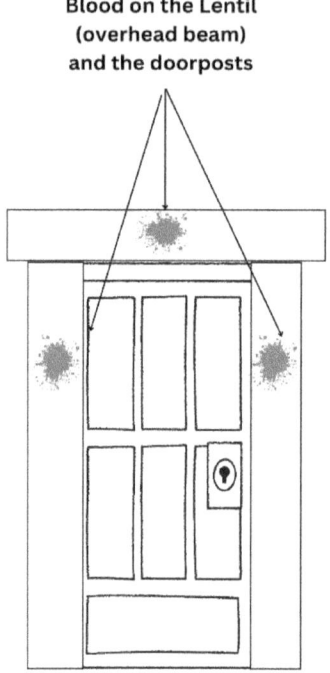

Thirteen-hundred years later, 30AD,[115] the Passover was again celebrated. For the spiritually acute Jews, the lamb was symbolic. It was to be spotless and flawless—a picture of sinlessness and perfection. It was to be sacrificed and its blood posted on the doorway—a picture of a perfect, sinless

---

[115] There are differing opinions among scholars as to the actual year, ranging from 30AD to 33 AD.

sacrifice made on behalf of all who came through the doorway. All those who sought this protection through the doorway would be shielded from God's wrath upon sinful mankind. For the Jews who had become numb to the Passover as an event that took place hundreds of years before, it was simply a wonderful time for family, food, and celebration.

Three years earlier when the Rescuer began His mission, the forerunner prophet[116] sent by God pointed Him out to his followers and said, "Look over there! That man is the **Passover Lamb** that has come from God to be sacrificed for us— for our sins and the sins of everyone in the world!" [117] With the Lamb of God (the Rescuer) attending this Passover, it was going to be unlike any other.

Leading up to this Passover, Satan had tried to kill the Rescuer many times, to stop Him from carrying out the prophetic event that would bruise the Rescuer's heel. Every time that the Jews tried to corner Him, trap Him, seize Him, or stone Him, He would somehow escape their attempt to end His life. He said, *"My time has not yet come."*[118] Satan even attempted to manipulate the Rescuer's followers into persuading Him to avoid being killed in the prescribed, preordained way.

---

[116] John the Baptist

[117] These are not John the Baptist's exact words, but the author's understanding of what John meant when he proclaimed, *"Behold, the Lamb of God who takes away the sin of the world!"* (John 1:29).

[118] *"So Jesus said to them, "**My time is not yet here**, but your time is always ready. ⁷ The world cannot hate you, but it hates Me because I testify about it, that its deeds are evil. ⁸ Go up to the feast yourselves; I am not going up to this feast, because **My time has not yet fully arrived***" (John 7:6-8).

127

*From that time Jesus began to point out to His disciples that it was necessary for Him to go to Jerusalem and to suffer many things from the elders, chief priests, and scribes, and to be killed, and to be raised up on the third day. ²² And yet Peter took Him aside and began to rebuke Him, saying, "God forbid it, Lord! This shall never happen to You!" ²³ But He turned and said to Peter, "**Get behind Me, Satan!** You are a stumbling block to Me; for you are not setting your mind on God's purposes, but men's."* (Matthew 16:21)

But now, it was **His time**. This was **His Passover**. It was time for **God's Lamb** to be sacrificed.

The first step, according to the process determined by Scripture, was that the Lamb had to be selected from the flock.[119]

This selection process began with the High Priest, Caiphas, when he made the statement that it was expedient for one man to die to save the many. From this point on, the religious leaders plotted to kill the Rescuer. Caiphas, representing the Jews, had made his choice—his pick of the Lamb that was to be killed.

*But one of them, Caiaphas, who was high priest that year, said to them, "You know nothing at all, ⁵⁰ nor are you taking into account that it is in your best interest that **one man die for the people**, and that the whole nation not perish instead." ⁵¹ Now he did not say this ⁽ᴵ⁾on his own, but as he was high priest that year, he prophesied that **Jesus was going to die** for the nation; ⁵² and not for the nation only but in order*

---

[119] *"Speak to all the congregation of Israel, saying, 'On the tenth of this month they are, each one, to take a lamb for themselves, according to the fathers' households, a lamb for each household'* (Exodus 12:3).

> *that He might also gather together into one the chil-*
> *dren of God who are scattered abroad.* John 11:49-
> 52

As Passover arrived, Satan moved to arrange for the acquisition of the Lamb by entering Judas, the betrayer, who
would deliver the Lamb to the High Priest.

> *Jesus then answered, "That man* (the one who was
> to betray Him) *is the one for whom I shall dip the*
> *piece of bread and give it to him." So when He had*
> *dipped the piece of bread, He took and gave it to Ju-*
> *das, the son of Simon Iscariot.* [27] *After this,* **Satan**
> **then entered him***. Therefore Jesus said to him, "What*
> *you are doing, do it quickly."* (John 13:26-27)

Next, the Passover process required that the lamb be in-
tensely examined to determine that it was without flaws. It
had to be spotless—perfect! The examination process of the
Rescuer began when an emergency meeting was declared in
the early morning hours on the eve of Passover and wasn't
concluded until the pronouncement by the final authority,
the Roman governor, Pontius Pilate.

The intense examination of God's Passover Lamb was conducted in six separate trials.

There were three religious trials:

1.	By Annas	John 18:12-23
2.	By Caiphas	Matthew 26:57-68
3.	By the entire Sanhedrin	Luke 22:66-71

There were three civil trials:

1. Before Pilate   John 18:28-38
2. Before Herod   Luke 23:1-7
3. Finally, the last and concluding
   trial before Pilate   Luke 23:11-16

After the final trial and review of all the facts, the pronouncement was made: the Rescuer had been found without flaws.

> *Now Pilate summoned to himself the chief priests, the rulers, and the people, [14] and he said to them, "You brought this man to me on the ground that he is inciting the people to revolt; and behold, after examining Him before you, I have found **no basis at all in the case of this man for the charges which you are bringing against Him.** [15] No, nor has Herod, for he sent Him back to us; and behold, nothing deserving death has been done by Him. (Luke 23:13-15)*

The last act of the Passover preparation was the slaughtering of the lamb. There was a pre-ordained, prescribed method by which **God's Lamb** was to be killed. The method was embedded in prophecy:

- He must be beaten, bloodied and pierced. Isaiah 53 (selected verses)

   > *But He was pierced for our offenses, He was crushed for our wrongdoings; The punishment for our well-being was laid upon Him But the Lord has caused the wrongdoing of us all To fall on Him. He was oppressed and afflicted, Yet He did not open His mouth; Like a lamb that is led to slaughter, And like a sheep that is silent before its shearers, So He did*

not open His mouth. By oppression and judgment He was taken away.

- He must be lifted up (raised up on a stake) like the bronzed serpent in the wilderness for all to see.

  And just as Moses lifted up the serpent in the wilderness, so must the Son of Man be lifted up, [15] so that everyone who believes will have eternal life in Him. (John 3:14-15)

- The process must be by crucifixion. Psalm 22[120] (selected verses)

  My God, my God, why have You forsaken me? But I am a worm and not a person, A disgrace of mankind and despised by the people. All who see me deride me; They sneer, they shake their heads, saying, "Turn him over to the Lord; let Him save him; Let Him rescue him, because He delights in him." They open their mouths wide at me, as a ravening and roaring lion. I am poured out like water, and all my bones are out of joint; My heart is like wax; It is melted within me. My strength is dried up like a piece of pottery, and my tongue clings to my jaws; For dogs have surrounded me; A band of evildoers has encompassed me; They pierced my hands and my feet. I can count all my bones. They

---

[120] The 22nd Psalm is a picture of a crucified man lifted up on a cross in agony, viewing the crowd below him shouting insults. This psalm was written almost 1000 years before the crucifixion of Jesus. When it was written, the process of crucifixion would not be developed by the Persians for another 600 years.

> *look, they stare at me; They divide my garments*
> *among them, and they cast lots for my clothing.*

- His heel must be bruised – a specific detail of Roman crucifixion in Judea at that time.

> *He shall crush you on the head, And you shall*
> ***bruise Him on the heel****.* (Genesis 3:15)

The drawings, paintings, statues, and images of Jesus on the cross show the Rescuer's feet in various positions, with most showing one foot overlapping the other with a single spike through both feet. How would the heel have been bruised in this configuration?

These figures and images are incorrect depictions of the crucifixion of Jesus. How do we know?

In 1968, archeologists discovered an ossuary[121] with the name "Yehohanan son of Hagkol" inscribed on the outside of the box. Inside the ossuary was the right heel bone of a man with an iron stake embedded in the bone. The discovery of this bone not only confirmed that the Romans did execute people in Judea (It had been previously contested there was no proof this form of execution was ever carried out in Judea.), but it also gave evidence of the specific process used to stake the feet to the cross. From this discovery, it is evident that each foot was impaled to the vertical post of the

---

[121] An ossuary is a "bone box" that was used to lovingly store the bones of a deceased family member. It was a memorial—a way of remembering a loved one who died.

cross, one on each side of the post, with a stake run through the heel.[122]

The nails were driven through
the heel bone of each foot.

Thus, was **God's Passover Lamb slaughtered.** This unique Passover was completed. The Rescuer's death fulfilled all the prophecies that were given in Scripture concerning the

---

[122] For photos of the heel bone and rusted stake, along with more detailed information, see https://www.ranker.com/list/stone-box-holds-only-trace-of-crucifixion/kellie-kreiss

sacrifice that would allow sinful men and women to approach the Most High and holy God. Yet, there remained one more prophesied event that had to take place. Without it, this sacrifice would have been meaningless and the Rescuer's mission a failure: the resurrection.

The **Resurrection of the Rescuer** was critical to the mission because

- It proved the sacrifice was acceptable to God—otherwise, mankind would be lost in sin (Romans 4:25; 1 Corinthians 15:14-19).

- It proved that Jesus was the prophesied *Holy One* who would never see bodily corruption (Psalm 16:10).

- It validated His own claims that He would be raised from the dead on the third day. If He did not rise, He would be a fraud (Mark 8:31; Matthew 17:22).

- It showed His triumph over death (1 John 5:11-12).

After the Rescuer's sacrificial death by the very means Satan tried to prevent, he could do nothing but watch helplessly as the Son rose on that third day as He said He would.

The Rescuer's mission was successfully completed. The Lamb of God was slaughtered. His heel was bruised with the spike that penetrated the heel bone and impaled His feet to the vertical post of the cross. He died six hours later, and His bloodied, beaten, and pierced body, with all bones intact (none were broken as prophesied) was placed in a grave, only to be raised from death on the third day. Satan's headship over humanity was crushed at the resurrection of the sacrificed Passover Lamb.

Now, those who have applied His blood to the doorposts and beam of their lives will be passed over when God pours out His wrath upon the unbelieving world of humanity that has rejected the One who came to rescue them.

"One hundred religious persons knit into a unity by careful organization do not constitute a church any more than eleven dead men make a football team."— A.W. Tozer

AUTHOR'S COMMENTS: Religion is man's attempt to reach God. It is a hopeless endeavor, regardless of the religious efforts of man. The gap is too great! Man's sin has created a gap that only God can bridge, which was accomplished by the prescribed sacrificial death of His Son. God built the bridge to us so that we can approach Him.

There is only one way to approach God: through His Son who said, *"I am **the Way**, the Truth and the Life. **No man** comes to the Father but **through Me!**"*[123] Jesus said that this one way is narrow and not many people find it.[124]

Religion falsely teaches that by being good enough God will accept us. Or, as some believe, that they are good enough because their "goods" outweigh their sins. These concepts are totally foreign to the Word of God, the Bible. The Bible tells us that *"all have sinned and fallen short of the glory of God."*[125] God's standard is sinless perfection, and **all** are disqualified from being with God due to their sins. No man is perfect. Not me or you.

---

[123] *"Jesus said to him, 'I am the way, and the truth, and the life; **no one comes to the Father except through Me**"* (John 14:6).

[124] *"Enter through the narrow gate; for the gate is wide and the way is broad that leads to destruction, and there are many who enter through it. 14 For the gate is **narrow and the way is constricted that leads to life, and there are few who find it**"* (Matthew 7:13-14).

[125] *"For all have sinned and fall short of the glory of God"* (Romans 3:23).

The teaching errors from religions are of the worst kind. Any denomination, sect, or group—even a "Christian" religion—that teaches that a person must make themselves righteous enough, perform certain religious activities and rituals, and work to make themselves acceptable to God are terribly wrong because they deny the totally sufficient work of the Son that He accomplished as the Lamb of God. People who follow this error by working hard to get to heaven are rejecting the Rescuer sent by God to rescue them.

The **only** compensation for sin that satisfied God's justice was a sinless, perfect sacrifice. The only One who could deliver that sacrifice was His Son who was *"tempted in all things just as we are, yet without sin."*[126] He was the only perfect sacrifice.

So, how is a person rescued? How is a person saved from God's wrath? It's not complicated.

- Believe **on** Him. Recognize and accept that He is who He claimed to be: fully God and fully man. Perfect. The Lamb of God.
- Trust that He died on your behalf – the sinless One for the sinful you!
- Believe that God raised Him from the dead and God accepted His death as full and complete payment for your sins.[127]
- Trust in Him and **Him alone** as your Rescuer and Savior. He is the object of your faith.

---

[126] *"For we do not have a high priest who cannot sympathize with our weaknesses, but One who has been tempted in all things just as we are, **yet without sin**"* (Hebrews 4:15).

[127] Some people believe they are, "too far gone," and it is impossible for God to accept them. This, too, is erroneous thinking. He **accepts all** who come to Him through His Son.

If you have trusted in Him, it is important to find a church that teaches the Bible. You may have to visit a few churches before you discover the one you like. However, when you do, start attending and gain as much information about God's Word as you can.

By the way, the *angel who would be God* will try to stop you. While you are a protected child of God now that you have trusted in His Son, Satan will want to discourage you from growing in God's grace.

Chapter 16

———⋅⋅⟨∞⟩ ⋅⋅———

Propaganda

"Propaganda does not deceive people; it merely helps them to deceive themselves."—Eric Hoffer

Definition: **Propaganda** – dissemination of information – facts, arguments, rumors, half-truths, or lies – to influence public opinion. It is often conveyed through mass media.[128]

After landing on Okinawa, the last island to be invaded five months before the surrender of Japan to American forces in September 1945, the U.S. infantry came across this message:–

American Officers and Men
We must express our deep regret over the death of President Roosevelt. The "American Tragedy" is now raised here at Okinawa with his death. You must have seen 70% of your CV's and 73% of your B's sink or be damaged causing 150,000 casualties. Not only the late President but anyone else would die in the excess of worry to hear such an annihilative damage. The dreadful loss that led your late leader to death will make you orphans on this island. The Japanese special attack corps will sink your vessels to the last

[128] Smith, B. L. (1999, July 26). *Propaganda*. Brittanica. Retrieved May 15, 2024, from https://www.britannica.com/topic/propaganda

destroyer. You will witness it realized in the near future.[129]

The Battle for Okinawa had just begun. With the amphibious landing, there was surprisingly little resistance. The Japanese infantry had adopted entirely different tactics since the early part of the war. Previously, Japan's generals had believed their own propaganda that their people were of a hardened, disciplined, and spiritually superior stock, whereas Western people were seen as corrupt and softened by prosperity, with no stomach for a difficult fight. They believed America would be easily defeated in open warfare and head-to-head battles. Banzai charges would overwhelm the U.S. infantrymen and prove the Japanese soldiers' loyalty to their Emperor-god.[130]

The propaganda sounded good, but the tide had turned, and Japan was losing the war. Starting with Iwo Jima, Japan's generals adopted a different tactic. Instead of head-to-head encounters with American forces, they pulled their troops into heavily fortified embankments, tunnels, and caves. Their goal now was not victory. Their navy was in shambles, and what few pilots they had left were inexperienced and easily downed by the new P-51 Mustang flown by savvy American fighter jockeys. The strength of America was pouring onto their beaches. Now, the tactic was to take as many Americans with them as they could.

---

[129] *Japanese propaganda leaflet recovered during the Battle of Okinawa.* Naval History and Heritage Command. Retrieved May 15, 2024, from https://www.history.navy.mil/content/history/nhhc/our-collections/artifacts/ephemera/letters/japanese-propaganda-leaflet--battle-of-okinawa.html

[130] The Emperor was considered to be a descendant from deity. It was considered a great honor to die for the Emperor.

The bloody battle for Okinawa had yet to be engaged. There would be battles on the island for significant territory – battles within the Battle. Hacksaw Ridge, Sugar Loaf, and Shuri Castle were but a few. To honor their god, the Japanese soldiers would keep fighting and take as many Americans with them on their trip to hell.

Such was the situation with Satan. After his defeat of Adam to gain god-of-this-world status, he started losing battle after battle to God until he lost the most significant battle in all of history. His defeat at Passover was the most significant one of all battles in the world, even surpassing the one to come at Armageddon. His headship and stranglehold on humanity were crushed by the Rescuer. The outcome of his war with God was determined at Passover. It was just a matter of time until the end. He would take as much of humanity with him on his trip to the burning lake of fire.

Satan's very first action following his defeat was on the day of the resurrection. His delegates, the chief priests, immediately published propaganda to deny that the event promised by the Rescuer took place.

> *Now while they were on their way, some of the men from the guard came into the city and reported to the chief priests all that had happened. 12 And when they had assembled with the elders and consulted together, they gave a large sum of money to the soldiers, 13 and said, "You are to say, 'His disciples came at night and stole Him while we were asleep.' 14 And if this comes to the governor's ears, we will appease him and [e]keep you out of trouble." 15 And they took the money and did as they had been instructed; and this story was widely spread among the Jews and is to this day.* (Matthew 28:11-15).

If you repeat a lie often enough, people will believe it, and you will even come to believe it yourself.— Joseph Goebbels, Nazi Propaganda Ministry

The reality of the resurrection was immediately attacked by Satan because this event is fundamental and critical to Christianity. In fact, the resurrection of the dead is not just a core belief; it is the basis upon which Christianity stands or falls!

One of the early attacks on Christianity was the claim that there would be no future resurrection of the dead by God. The believers in Corinth wrote to the Apostle Paul questioning whether there would be a resurrection because some people had come into the church claiming this event would not take place. Paul's letter back to the church at Corinth stated this astounding truth:

> *Now if Christ is preached, that He has been raised from the dead, how do some among you say that there is no resurrection of the dead?* [13] *But if there is no resurrection of the dead, then not even Christ has been raised;* [14] *and if Christ has not been raised, then our preaching is in vain, your faith also is in vain.* [15] *Moreover, we are even found to be false witnesses of God, because we testified [g]against God that He raised [h]Christ, whom He did not raise, if in fact the dead are not raised.* [16] *For if the dead are not raised, then not even Christ has been raised;* [17] *and if Christ has not been raised, your faith is worthless; you are still in your sins.* [18] *Then also those who have fallen asleep in Christ have perished.* [19] *If we have hoped in Christ only in this life, we are of all people most to be pitied.* (1 Corinthians 15:12-19)

The Apostle Paul stated in his letter to the Corinthians that to deny the future, physical, bodily resurrection of the dead was to deny the resurrection of Jesus—and to deny the bodily resurrection of Jesus would be to declare their faith was of no value. If their faith had no value, then no salvation is acquired by trusting in the death, burial, and resurrection of Christ—if He, in fact, wasn't resurrected. The conclusion is that believers would still be as they were before Christ: lost in their sins, lost to God, and destined for hell. Not only that but all their relatives who died believing in Christ would also be lost. Finally, the apostles of Jesus would be greatly pitied, since they dedicated their lives to a false hope beyond the grave.

The Apostle Paul, in his letter to the Corinthians, stated that there will be a bodily resurrection. He gave evidence of the resurrection of Christ to prove it. He visited, spoke to, and ate with many people after His resurrection. These people touched, hugged, and felt Him. Thomas put his fingers into the smaller wounds and his whole hand into the gaping side wound where the spear was thrust. When Paul wrote this letter, he spoke of the 500 people who were eyewitness to the resurrected Christ and that many of them were still alive and could be interviewed to validate this truth.[131]

With a little investigative work regarding Satan's propaganda produced by the chief priests, it is easy to see it for the lie that it is. The key is this event recorded in Matthew 27:62-66.

> *Now on the next day, that is, the day which is after the preparation, the chief priests and the Pharisees gathered together with Pilate, ⁶³ and they said, "Sir, we remember that when that deceiver was still alive, He said, 'After three days I am rising.' ⁶⁴ Therefore, give orders for the*

---

[131] The entire chapter of 1 Corinthians 15 covers this topic in detail.

> *tomb to be made secure until the third day; otherwise, His disciples may come and steal Him, and say to the people, 'He has risen from the dead,' and the last deception will be worse than the first."* [65] *Pilate said to them, "You have a **guard**; go, make it as secure as you know how."* [66] *And they went and made the tomb **secure with the guard, sealing the stone.***

A Roman guard, known as a watch, was set at the tomb. The seal of Rome was on the covering stone to secure the opening. The Roman watch consisted of sixteen armed soldiers, with four on duty and twelve off duty. The off-duty soldiers had to remain in the immediate vicinity of the target they were guarding (in this case, the tomb). In the event of an attack, the unit swelled to an incredibly effective fighting force of sixteen of the best-trained soldiers in the world.[132]

To claim that a motley band of terrified fishermen (who had the day before fled from capture at the garden) would dare to take on the Roman watch and break the seal of Rome[133] to retrieve the body of a dead leader is absurd. Had there been a successful attack by the fishermen, there would have been at least some badly wounded or dead soldiers, as well as severe casualties among the fishermen. But there was no evidence of a fight.

The very guard that the religious leaders demanded from Pilate to prevent the body from being stolen by the disciples became the best evidence that the body was not stolen!

As Matthew stated in 28:15, the false narrative persisted until the day his gospel was penned. That same lie continues

---

[132] McDowell, J. (1981). *The Resurrection Factor* (p. 56). Here's Life Publishers, San Bernadino, CA.

[133] An act punishable by death.

into the 21st century. One can add a number of equally pre-posterous theories about what might have happened after the burial of the Rescuer, all attempting to deny His physical, bodily resurrection.

Here are a few:

- The Swoon Theory – Jesus didn't die on the cross. He passed out, and the guards thought that He was dead. He was taken down from the cross and buried in the tomb. Later, He recovered from His injuries, escaped from the tomb, and then appeared to His disciples.

- The Faked Death Theory – much like the Swoon Theory, except Jesus was conscious and pretended to be dead. The guards took Him down from the cross and gave Him over to His people. He recovered from His injuries and then appeared to His disciples.

- Mistaken Identity Theory – it wasn't Jesus who died, but someone who looked just like Him was crucified in His place. After the crucifixion, He appeared to His followers, and they declared He had risen from the dead.

  This theory is similar to the one espoused by Islam. The Qu'ran (Koran) states:

  *And [for] their saying, "Indeed, we have killed the Messiah, Jesus, the son of Mary, the messenger of Allah." And **they did not kill him**, nor did they **crucify him**; but [another] **was made to resemble him** to them. And indeed, those who differ over it are in doubt about it. They have no knowledge of it except* *the following of assumption. And they did not kill him, for certain.* Qu'ran 4:157

- The Spiritual Resurrection Theory – Jesus died a physical death, but His resurrection was spiritual. His disciples saw Jesus' spirit.

Other theories have been developed over the years to attack the very foundation of Christianity. This propaganda of Satan is easily accepted by people who choose not to investigate the source of truth—God's Word, the Bible.

Satan continues his fight to take as many people to the gates of hell with him as he can. It will be seen in future chapters that as his time grows short, Satan's fury and the intensity of his attacks on mankind will accelerate in both quantity and intensity.

Chapter 17

Infiltrate

"The Revolution won't happen with guns, rather it will happen incrementally, year by year, generation by generation. We will gradually infiltrate their educational institutions and their political offices, transforming them slowly into Marxist entities as we move towards universal egalitarianism."—Max Horkheimer

No military examples from history are needed. The world only has to look at the state of America. A small group of businessmen sitting in a restaurant were overheard talking as they ate. "What is happening to America? Our country is falling apart. We have been divided. It all happened so fast."

No, not really. It didn't happen fast. It took decades. Slowly, the foundation of America has been eaten away. When the covers are pulled away, a foundation of wormwood is revealed. The once stout financial, moral, societal, and spiritual legs upon which the country was built are now full of holes– a country on the verge of collapse.

History will show that infiltration and the transformation of its foundational areas were the reasons America was lost.

Satan used infiltration long before the Marxists began assaulting America from within.

When the Rescuer was presented to the people as their king, they rejected Him.

> *But Pilate, wanting to release Jesus, addressed them again, ²¹ but they kept on crying out, saying, "Crucify, crucify Him!"* (Luke 23:20-21)

After the rejection of the Rescuer by Israel, an entirely new entity was born. The birth took place on Pentecost—fifty days after the Resurrection—when the Holy Spirit descended upon a group of followers.[134] This was the birth of the church. His church. This new organization was not a building but a spiritual brotherhood of men and women who believed on Him,[135] who were forgiven,[136] and who were sealed by the Holy Spirit[137] as a guarantee of their eternal destiny with their Rescuer in heaven. This fellowship has members throughout the world. While the members belong to local churches of which there are thousands, they are part

---

[134] *"When the day of Pentecost [a]had come, they were all together in one place. ² And suddenly a noise like a violent rushing wind came from heaven, and it filled the whole house where they were sitting. ³ And tongues that looked like fire appeared to them, [b]distributing themselves, and a tongue [c]rested on each one of them"* (Acts 2:1-3).

[135] *"Therefore they said to Him, "What are we to do, so that we may accomplish the works of God?" ²⁹ Jesus answered and said to them, "This is the work of God, that you **believe in Him** whom He has sent"* (John 6:28-29).

[136] *"Therefore there is now **no condemnation** at all for those who are in Christ Jesus"* (Romans 8:1).

[137] *"In[/]Him, you also, after listening to the message of truth, the gospel of your salvation—having also believed, you were **sealed in Him with the Holy Spirit** of the promise"* (Ephesians 1:13).

of this single entity known to God as His church, *the body of Christ.* [138]

Prior to the birth of the church, Israel was God's vehicle to make Himself known to the world. With the rejection of the Rescuer and the birth of the church, Israel was no longer the entity God used to evangelize people and nations. The evangelical baton was taken from Israel and given to the church.[139] The church became the offense, the force that would carry the Word of God to the ends of the earth.

The church became the greatest enemy of Satan. Satan's mission is to take as many people as possible with him to his ultimate destination of hell. However, the church is diametrically opposite. The mission of the church is to bring the gospel (which means Good News!)—the Good News of the Rescuer—to tell the world of His rescue mission. It is to offer the people of the world God's grace through His sacrificial work on the cross on their behalf.

Satan's plan of attack against the church began almost immediately. The church was born on Pentecost. Satan's plan

---

[138] While a religious organization may declare itself as a church, it is the Holy Spirit who is resident within the body of believers that identifies it as a church of Jesus Christ.

[139] "So, when they had come together, they *began* asking Him, saying, 'Lord, is it at this time that You are **restoring the kingdom to Israel**?' [7] But He said to them, "It is not for you to know periods of time or appointed times which the Father has set by His own authority; [8] but you will receive power when the Holy Spirit has come upon you; and **you shall be My witnesses both in Jerusalem and in all Judea, and Samaria, and as far as the remotest part of the earth**" (Acts 1:6-8).

was developed on Pentecost-plus-one. His plan included *"deceitful spirits and the doctrine of demons."* [140]

The action points of Satan's plan include:

- The development of doctrines (principles and teachings) that will slightly modify, confuse, or conflict with the teaching from the Bible.
- The infiltration of this new entity, the church, and once inside, attack it at its foundation.
- The continual corruption of its foundation with false teaching until the church is so odious to the believers they leave to find a new church where the foundation is solid and secure.

The doctrine of demons includes teachings specifically mentioned in Scripture such as forbidding marriage to a group or individual or requiring that the congregation abstain from eating certain foods. In a larger context, these demonic doctrines attack the person and work of the Rescuer. Some demonic doctrines deny that the resurrection of the Rescuer ever took place, while others teach that the sacrifice of the Rescuer was not fully sufficient. They teach that to gain eternal life, additional work or effort is required by the believer.

Other teachings developed by deceitful spirits demand that a person must work to maintain the salvation earned by the Lamb of God. These demonic spirits also offer idols or statues as objects of their faith. Charms, special medals, and prayers to people who have died are included in their arsenal of false doctrine.

---

[140] *"But the Spirit explicitly says that in later times some will [a]fall away from the faith, paying attention to deceitful spirits and teachings of demons"* (1 Timothy 4:1).

With an opposing or "one-off" doctrinal package, infiltration of the church by these demons of Satan is accomplished by using intelligent people who have a good knowledge of the Bible. These people can use their background and speaking skills to be invited to teach and even preach from the pulpit. After the infiltrators have gained the confidence of the congregation, they'll move to become leaders in the church. As deacons, elders, and worship leaders of the church, they can change the foundational doctrine that established the church. The believers will find themselves shocked at the new practices and leave this spiritually decrepit organization.

After the believers depart, false teachers will occupy the church facility and open its doors to all forms of religious activities. While quoting selected passages from the Bible, they will carefully avoid the clear, saving message of the Rescuer. These leaders will work to make the people feel very satisfied that they are spiritual, and they are doing the work of God. The pastors and leaders will keep the people busy with good social activities that are very "Christian": food drives for the poor, men's fellowship groups and ladies' book studies. For Sunday worship services, they will provide outstanding entertainment with good Christian music, excellent singers, and a good background musical band or ensemble. It will all feel so good, but the message of the Passover victory will play a minor role, or avoided at all costs.

With these "upgrades," another church body of believers will have been transformed into just another church building owned by Satan! Time for Satan's tools to move on to infiltrate another church. These attacks of infiltration on the body of believers started immediately after the birth of the church in Jerusalem and continue today, all over the world.

> *"Children, it is the last hour; and just as you heard that **antichrist** is coming, even now many **antichrists***

have appeared; from this we know that it is the last hour"[141] (1 John 2:18).

Immediately after Pentecost, in parallel with his plan to infiltrate churches with the doctrine of demons, Satan also introduced the system of the antichrist, a precurser to the person called the antichrist. The antichrist is a person, a man who will one day rise to oppose the Rescuer when He returns.[142] The work of the antichrist will be limited to little more than seven years when he appears on the earth. The work of the system of the antichrist began immediately after the birth of the church and continues to plague not just the church but the world.

Many scholars and teachers of Scripture understand that this future battle between the returning Rescuer and the antichrist will take place at or near a location in Israel called Armageddon. God alone will signal when this battle is to occur, and only God knows that day. To prepare for this battle, throughout history, Satan has had this chess piece in his arsenal waiting to be played. He has always had one man prepared to be introduced to the world as his antichrist. Today, in Satan's inventory, a man is waiting to be released onto the world with all the characteristics of the antichrist described in the Bible.

In addition to the antichrist (the man), there is also a system or spirit of the antichrist. Like the man – the antichrist – this system opposes all that Christ has done, what He is doing in

---

[141] After the birth of the church on Pentecost, a new spiritual age began called the church age, also known as the age of grace. This age is referred to in Scripture as *the last hour.*

[142] Jesus Christ promised His church that He will return, first for them, then to confront the evil world system of the antichrist at Armageddon. This return will be addressed in the last chapters of this book.

the world, and all He will do upon His return. This conflict can be seen today. Christ and the Bible point mankind to see God in creation. However, the spirit of the antichrist points mankind to see the source of their creation in a primordial pool of random muck. The heavens declare the glory of God, as seen in the Hubble and Webb telescopes, but the spirit of the antichrist points man to theories concluding that the universe created itself. An article from Reuters news quoted physicist Stephen Hawking:

> *Because there is a law such as gravity, the universe can and will* **create itself from nothing**. *Spontaneous creation is the reason there is something rather than nothing, why the universe exists, why we exist," Hawking writes. "It is not necessary to invoke God to light the blue touch paper and set the universe going.[143]*

The two-pronged message of the spirit of the antichrist to mankind is this:

1. You don't need to believe in a creator because there has never been one. Because there was never a creator, there is no majestic, holy, omnipotent being. Because there was never a creator to sin against, there was never a need for a Rescuer. When your time clock on Earth makes its final tick, you will become one with the cosmos.

   The nitrogen in our DNA, the calcium in our teeth, the iron in our blood, the carbon in our apple pies

---

[143] Holden, M. (n.d.). *God Did Not Create the Universe, says Hawking.* Reuters.com. Retrieved May 10, 2024, from https://www.reuters.com/article/idUSTRE6811FN/

were made in the interiors of collapsing stars. We are made of star stuff."—Carl Sagan, Cosmos

2. If you do need a god, there is a smorgasbord of choices. Pick a religion. It doesn't matter which one: Hinduism, Islam, Christianity, Shinto, whatever. There are many paths to your god. Choose a religious belief that will make you comfortable, and you can create the characteristics of the god you seek to worship.

Although the war was lost at Passover, Satan's ongoing attack on humanity to take as many with him as he can continues. The ongoing message of the spirit of the antichrist to mankind seeks to override the voice of creation shouting the existence of the Most High God. Satan seeks to destroy the fellowship of those who have heard and responded to the shout of creation by approaching the Creator through the work of the Passover Lamb on the cross. He does so through infiltration by his agents teaching the doctrine of demons.

Will Satan's attacks ever end?

Chapter 18

⸻⸺◦⟨∞⟩◦⸺⸻

Hated Among Nations

"If the Arabs put down their weapons today, there would be no more violence. If the Jews put down their weapons today, there would be no more Israel."—Golda Meir

In the spring of 1948, the Thirteen Leaders voted on the name of the independent state to be used when their Declaration of Independence was proclaimed. Only two names were considered. One name was Zion and the other Israel![144]

A little over a week later, on May 15, 1948, David Ben-Gurion, leader of the new Jewish state, took the microphone in the new little country's fledgling radio station to announce to the world the establishment of the independent state of Israel. As he read the words of Israel's Declaration of Independence, he recalled in his diary, "There was no joy in my heart. I was thinking of only one thing, the war we were going to have to fight."[145]

Ben-Gurion was right. As the bright white flag with the sky-blue imprint of the Star of David was raised in conjunction with the declaration, Israel had painted a large bullseye on itself, and the world was watching. General Satan was watching too. He always despised the Jews. With the birth

---

[144] Collins, L., & Lapierre, D. (1988). *O Jerusalem.* Simon & Schuster, New York., p. 56

[145] Ibid, p. 382

of their new nation, he became an instant Israel-hater as well. General Satan set his field glasses down and immediately stirred up four Arab armies and their air forces (armed with then-modern-day weapons and fighter planes from the recently concluded Second World War) and put them on the move to destroy the brand-new nation.

> *The war started on the first night of the* state's *existence. The Israel Defense Force (IDF) was only just getting organized and seriously lacked guns and ammunition. It had to fight the Arab invaders with almost no means. According to the Arab plan, the Egyptian army was supposed to conquer the Jewish settlements in the Negev, move on to Ashkelon, to Ashdod, and then reach Tel Aviv. The Syrian, Lebanese and Iraqi armies were supposed to move through the Yizre'el Valley and reach Haifa.*[146]

The plans of the Arab combined armies were never accomplished. Somehow, some way, Israel survived its first days as a nation. That was 75 years ago.

The world wondered how that little country, with many of Europe's Jews who survived the Holocaust as the newest citizens of the newest nation, survived that first year. The world wonders how it not only survives but prospers in today's world—when the world hates Jews and their nation, Israel. It is the most hated among all nations of the world. We even have a special word in our dictionary to describe the bias against these people and this nation. The dictionary (dictionary.com) defines antisemitism as *hostility to, or prejudice against Jewish people.*

---

[146] Mishal, N. (2008). *Israel 60 - Those Were The Years* (p. 17). Miskal-Publishing and Distribution, Ltd., Tel-Aviv.

Within the U.S. State Department, there is a special envoy office to combat antisemitism. They have even developed a *working definition* of antisemitism.

> *Antisemitism is a certain perception of Jews, which may be expressed as hatred toward Jews. Rhetorical and physical manifestations of antisemitism are directed toward Jewish or non-Jewish individuals and/or their property, toward Jewish community institutions and religious facilities.[147]*

There is no contest. Jews are the most despised and persecuted people in the world. A short study of history reveals the truth of this conclusion.

- Ancient persecution can be found in the apocryphal documents such as First and Second Maccabees, where the Greeks martyred Jews for their refusal to abandon dietary regulations contained in the Law of Moses.

- In the centuries after the beginning of Christianity, the Jews who did not convert in the regions of the Roman Empire were increasingly rejected, especially when Rome became a Christian empire. Frequently, the Romans categorized the Jews as *"Christ killers" and held them as responsible as their ancestors for the execution of Jesus Christ.[148]*

---

[147] *Defining Antisemitism.* U.S. Department of State. Retrieved October 22, 2024, from https://www.state.gov/defining-antisemitism/

[148] Moran, F. (n.d.). *History of Jewish Persecution | Antisemitism, Reasons & Problems.* Study.com. Retrieved October 22, 2024, from https://study.com/academy/lesson/history-of-jewish-persecution.html

- During the Crusades, the Jews were zealously persecuted and massacred throughout Western Europe.[149]

- It has been estimated that during the Holocaust of
World War II over 6 million Jews were murdered by
the Nazi "Final Solution" killing machine.

Today, the tiny nation of Israel is held in great disdain by the
world's governmental organizations. The United Nations
seems to take great pleasure in passing resolutions aimed at
condemning Israel for its actions or practices, while ignoring
other countries with similar (or worse) activities.

*The UN General Assembly rebuked Israel on Tues-
day in three separate resolutions, concluding the
world body's 2023 legislation with a total of 14 resolutions that single out the Jewish state, and seven
on the rest of the world combined. There was one
resolution each adopted yesterday for the regimes of
North Korea, Iran, Syria and Myanmar, and one on
Russia's violations in Crimea. Earlier in the year,
there was one resolution deploring Russian aggression in Ukraine, and one condemning the U.S. for its
embargo of Cuba.[150]*

---

[149] (1984). *Studies in Church History, Volume 21: Persecution and Toleration* (pp. 51-72). W.J. Sheils, Editor.

[150] *UN General Assembly condemns Israel 14 times in 2023, rest of world
7*. U.N. Watch. Retrieved May 26, 2024, from https://unwatch.org/un-
general-assembly-condemns-israel-14-times-in-2023-rest-of-world-
7/#:~:text=NEW%20YORK%2C%20December%2020%2C%202023,r
est%20of%20the%20world%20combined.

There is no rationale, no logical explanation for the intense hatred of Jews and the nation of Israel. Why the burning abhorrence? Where do we look for an answer?

The answer is in the Bible, and it can be found in Revelation Chapter 12.

Theodore Epp, author of a commentary on the book of Revelation, made the following statement:

> *One cannot understand the entire Book of Revelation unless he understands the 12th chapter. The truth revealed in Revelation reaches backward to Abraham* (the Father of the Jews) *and forward to the end of the Tribulation* (a prophesied end-time event).[151] Epp went on to state: *Revelation 12 reveals the conflict of the ages. This conflict involves Israel, Christ and Satan.*[152]

Humanity's attacks on Jews and the nation of Israel can be traced to the hatred that continually emanates from Satan. He hates Abraham's lineage, the Jews, and the nation of the Jews because he hates Christ and God. This principle is clearly demonstrated in the first six verses of Revelation Chapter 12, which is stated in allegory form as a sign in heaven.

> *A great **sign appeared in heaven**: a woman clothed with the sun, and the moon under her feet, and on her head a crown of twelve stars; and she was pregnant*

---

[151] Epp, T. H. (1969). *Practical Studies in Revelation, Vol II*. The Good News Broadcasting Association, Inc., Lincoln, Ne., p162

[152] ibid. p 163

and she cried out, being in labor and in pain to give birth.

*³ Then another **sign appeared in heaven**: and behold, a great red dragon having seven heads and ten horns, and on his heads were seven crowns. ⁴ And his tail swept away a third of the stars of heaven and hurled them to the earth. And the dragon stood before the woman who was about to give birth, so that when she gave birth he might devour her Child.*

⁵ And she gave birth to a Son, a male, who is going to rule all the nations with a rod of iron; and her Child was caught up to God and to His throne. ⁶ Then the woman fled into the wilderness where she had a place prepared by God, so that there she would be nourished for 1,260 days. (Revelation 12:1-6)

There are two allegories (signs) in the picture given in the above verses: the dragon and the woman. The identity of the dragon is Satan as defined in Scripture a few verses later in the same chapter:

*And **the great dragon** was thrown down, the serpent of old **who is called the devil and Satan**, who deceives the whole world; he was thrown down to the earth, and his angels were thrown down with him.* (Revelation 12:9)

Only the identity of the woman remains. Once her identity is found, the child's identity will be determined. Through the careful study of Scripture, the Bible reveals that the woman is Israel.[153] The male child that the nation of Israel (the

---

[153] See Author's Comments at the end of this chapter.

woman) delivers is the Rescuer.[154] With the correct identity of the dragon (Satan), the woman (Israel), and the male child (the Rescuer), Revelation Chapter 12 is communicating to the reader that the world's hatred of Israel (the nation of twelve stars/Twelve Tribes of Jacob (aka Israel)) is the result of the dragon's desire to kill the seed (the offspring) of Abraham (Father of the Jews). It is Abraham's seed who was prophesied to one day bless all the nations of the world.

> *And in your seed all the nations of the earth shall be blessed, because you have obeyed My voice.* (Genesis 22:18)

This unfulfilled prophecy states that the seed of Abraham will one day sit on the throne of the world. Through this ruler, the nations of the world will be blessed – the world will finally have peace.

Here then is the source of Satan's hatred of the Jew and his continuing attacks against Israel. Here is the reason that millions of Jews have been murdered. This is why Jews will remain the most despised of all peoples. This is why Israel will, until the Rescuer sits on the throne, be in turmoil. The Rescuer, a Jew, the King of the Jews, the King of Israel, and Prince of Peace will occupy the throne Satan has so desperately struggled to protect. This is why the dragon (Satan) sought to devour/kill the Child of Israel.

God has promised Israel and the world that a day is coming when an offspring of King David (a Jew) will sit on the throne as King. It will be a kingdom unlike any other because it will be established by God. In addition, the kingdom (and king) will be eternal! This promise is known as the Davidic

---

[154] Same as above

Covenant that was made during the time of David. God made the following promise to David, which remains unfulfilled.

> *I will raise up your descendant after you, who will come from you, and **I will establish his king-dom**. [13] He shall build a house for My name, and I will establish the throne of his kingdom **forever**.* (2 Samuel 7:12)

Until then, Satan's attacks on Israel continue as before and will continue until the final battle is decided between the forces of Satan and the forces of the Rescuer.

This future, final battle is known as Armageddon.

AUTHOR'S COMMENTS: Despite the many paintings and icons appearing in Roman Catholic churches and literature that claim Mary is the woman in Revelation Chapter 12, Scripture clearly reveals the identity of the "woman" who gave birth to the male Child as someone else. It is important to note that the Bible speaks of the woman as a **sign**, indicating that the vision is not human but is an allegory that represents something else.

> *A **great sign** appeared in heaven: a woman clothed with the sun, and the moon under her feet, and on her head a crown of twelve stars.* (Revelation 12:1)

In searching for an understanding of an allegory in the Bible, opinions have no bearing when the Bible gives the meaning. The Bible is its own best interpreter. One can have 100 percent confidence in the meaning when a biblical reference can be found for the symbolism used. In the case of the woman as a symbol, Genesis Chapter 37 reveals one of Joseph's dreams in which we find the sun, moon, and twelve stars (where Joseph, the dreamer, is the 12th star).

> *Behold, I have had yet another dream; and behold, the sun and the moon, and eleven stars were bowing down to me." 10 He also told it to his father as well as to his brothers; and his father rebuked him and said to him, "What is this dream that you have had? Am I and your mother and your brothers actually going to come to bow down to the ground before you?* (Genesis 37:9-10)

Joseph's father Jacob (Remember, God changed Jacob's name to **Israel**.) is the sun in the allegory. His wife Rachel is the moon, and his brothers and he are the twelve stars (or tribes) of Jacob/Israel. Jacob clearly understands the dream and is upset at the thought that the parents would bow down to their offspring. He expresses his displeasure. Later in the chapter, it is evident that Joseph's brothers also understood the dream and were very angry with him.

From this passage, the "woman" clothed with Israel and the twelve tribes is the nation of Israel, which birthed the male child (the Messiah, Jesus). The dragon (Satan) sought to devour (kill) the child. (This has always been the objective of Satan in the Seed-Kill Campaign – to destroy the seed of the woman that would crush his head.)

A further indication that the "woman" is Israel and not Mary is that the woman runs in fear to the wilderness and is protected for 1260 days (or 3 ½ years), which is the latter half of the tribulation period known as, "The Time of Jacob's Trouble."[155] It is during this time that Israel (the "woman"

---

[155] See Matthew 24:15-22 and Jeremiah 30:7

of Revelation Chapter 12) will be persecuted with extreme cruelty by Satan's antichrist.

> *And she gave birth to a Son, a male, who is going to rule all the nations with a rod of iron; and her Child was caught up to God and to His throne. [6] Then the* **woman fled into the wilderness** *where she had a place prepared by God, so that there she would be nourished for* **1,260 days**. (Revelation 12:5-6)

Chapter 19

Something Wicked

"We desperately need to understand something of the magnitude of sin, of evil, and of gross wickedness in this world if we are to appreciate our redemption. God's love, grace, and mercy shine all the brighter against the awful reality of evil. Indeed, the very existence of evil is a powerful proof of God's existence and holiness."—Dave Hunt

The three witches circled the bubbling cauldron, each taking a turn to add a hideous component to the witches' brew. As each witch took her turn dropping her offering into the black liquid, she gave a rhythmic chant. After multiple iterations, it was the second witch who cast the final ingredient into the pot. As she did, she declared the final rhyme.

> *By the pricking of my thumb,*
> ***Something Wicked*** *this way comes.*[156]

It doesn't depend on religious belief, nationality, race, gender, language or any other demographic. Talk with anyone about how they feel about the world we live in today, and the response is generally the same. Not good. Talk further to explore the reasons for their evaluation. What is revealed is there is a sense something is very wrong—the world seems

---

[156] MacBeth, Act 4, Scene 1. A play by William Shakespeare. Retrieved October 22, 2024, from, https://www.folger.edu/explore/shakespeares-works/macbeth/read/4/1/

to be spinning out of control, and something bad, very bad is going to happen.

Today, the sense that something wicked is coming seems to be a common fear expressed by people. There is a loss of confidence in virtually everything people have trusted. Stable, effective governments have become a thing of the past, having been replaced by monstrous bureaucracies that cannot function due to their own sizes. Power generation systems have become inadequate for worldwide energy demands. Major moves to rapidly create new sources that meet stringent environmental requirements are proving to be less than ideal. Artificial intelligence weaponry, pilotless fighter jets, and robotic soldiers coupled with the growing movement of world powers to place nuclear weapons in space present ever-changing attacks on the confidence of people in their nation's security.

Economies are straining and struggling. The mighty American dollar, the worldwide medium of exchange, has only marginal relative strength as American debt has soared, and inflation has devalued the buying power of this once-strong currency. Worldwide, people are investing in bitcoin, priced at levels that are staggering, considering there are no hard assets or a taxing base to support the valuation. It is simply digital money with nothing behind it. Yet, in many cases, people are putting more confidence in this digital coinage than the currency of their own governments!

People are worried and are seeing situations they have never witnessed before. The level of governmental control is rapidly expanding in technologically advanced nations around the world. In America, printed money and coinage as stores of value are disappearing with the digitizing of the supply of money. Purchases are made for groceries, office supplies, clothing, books, appliances, and even automobiles using credit and debit cards, and payments are now made using the ever-powerful cell phone. Monthly utility bills are automatically deducted by vendors from customers' checking accounts or posted to debit or credit cards. As hard currency disappears, people are becoming increasingly aware that family spending will be easily monitored and controlled by governmental agencies when, not if, the decision is made.

On the world political stage, Russia invaded its neighbor, Ukraine, with the objective of absorbing the country and its people into Putin's desire for an empire. NATO countries are banding together in an attempt to contain Russia's expansionary ideas by supporting Ukraine in its war with Russia. Communist China is building islands in the South China Sea with the goal of controlling shipping in Asian markets, while simultaneously threatening to invade Taiwan and bringing its government under the control of the Communist Chinese Party. Iran continues its export of terror to their Middle East terrorist agencies of Hamas, Hezbollah, and others, with the ultimate goal of wiping out Israel.

The song, "Imagine," was written by John Lennon about a dreamer visualizing a better world. He imagined that the people of the world could obliterate all obstacles to peace. In Lennon's imagined world, there were no countries (no borders) so that there wouldn't be wars between nations. He dreamed that there was no afterlife (no heaven, no hell), which meant that there would be no need for religions and thus, no wars between people of different religions. His song has become a worldwide hymn for peace.

Today, fifty-three years after the release of the song, it still resonates with people. Thousands still pour onto the streets of cities around the world, carrying flags of peace and singing Lennon's song. People are singing, crying and praying for peace. Are there any people of any nation, religion, or background who don't desire peace for their families and loved ones? Then why can't we have peace? We have gone through two world wars, each ending with the hope this last war will be the last war. Yet, conflict continually breaks out in some part of the world.

All these worldwide social, political, (im)moral, and financial pressures are causing changes. There is a general movement toward globalism. The thought is that if there is a unifying super government that rules over all the governments of the world, then this control would bring an end to wars. This government would function as the United Nations but with full authority to enforce its decisions upon any country or world system that gets out of line.

With one entity controlling the world's economies, poverty would be eliminated by the balancing of wealth so no one nation is richer or poorer than another. It all sounds so good!

Satan's cauldron of evil works is cooking as the world moves ever closer to the end-time events recorded by the Apostle John in the book of Revelation.

Jesus spoke of this time when He told His disciples:

> *For then there will be a **great tribulation**, such as has not occurred since the beginning of the world until now, nor ever will again. [22] And if those days had not been cut short, **no life would have been saved**; but for the sake of the elect those days will be cut short.* (Matthew 24:21-22)

The stage has been set for Satan's greatest attack on mankind. Something wicked is surely coming this way.

Chapter 20

The Chess Board

"Pawns; they are the soul of chess: it is they alone that determine the attack and the defense, and the winning or losing of the game depends entirely on their good or bad arrangement."—François-André Danican Philidor

Before it happened, the chessboard was competitively uneven. On one side, there were only two white pieces remaining: the queen and the king. The opposite side of the board had the full array of dark pieces: the king, queen, rooks, knights, bishops, and pawns. Interestingly, on the dark side, some pieces were black, others dark grey, and still others varying shades of grey.

Then something happened. A very significant, yet unknown event occurred, causing the board to be knocked off the table and the pieces scattered.

When the board was reset for the players, an entirely different layout of the opposing pieces was displayed.

On the white side, only the king remained. The powerful queen had disappeared; she couldn't be found and seemed to have vanished in mid-air. On the dark side, there were thirteen pieces—powerful pieces. There were no shades of gray in them. They were of the deepest and darkest black pigment on the color chart. The black pieces were somehow all enormously powerful. Unlike in a normal chess game, all the pawns were as large and powerful as those in the back row, except for one. There was one little pawn so small that it seemed insignificant.

The book of Revelation, starting in Chapter 4, tells of "*the things which will take place,*" [157] the things to come. The future. It shows us the world *chessboard* after some significant event has caused a complete rearrangement of world powers.

Today, prior to this unknown, world-changing event, the white player is down to two pieces: Israel (the white king) and the most powerful piece on any chess board, the white queen (the Rescuer's church). These are the only pieces remaining. The white queen, although shrinking in size over the years, still retains the power of the Holy Spirit, for it is the Spirit that lives inside of each born-again believer that comprises the church of the Rescuer. The white king, Israel (the nation, the people and the land) is on the board, still waiting for its Messiah but refusing to recognize the kingship of the Rescuer. The powerful queen remains fixated upon protecting the king because she recognizes that the Rescuer will one day occupy the throne of David—King of Israel!

The dark side of the board prior to the big-impact event consisted of pieces in varying shades, from medium grey to dark

---

[157] John the Apostle describes the Rescuer's appearing to him, over fifty years after the resurrection. "*When I saw Him, I fell at His feet like a dead man. And He placed His right hand on me, saying, "Do not be afraid; I am the first and the last, [18] and the living One; and I was dead, and behold, I am alive forevermore, and I have the keys of death and of Hades. [19] Therefore write the things which you have seen, [a]and the things which are, and* **the things which will take place** *after these things*" (Revelation 1:17-19).

black. Some of the pieces are the Western nations that have historically stood with Israel but are becoming questionable allies under the influence of the black king (Satan). America, a once all-in friend and promoter of the nation surrounded by enemies and former enemies, now plays Israel as a political hot potato, shifting it from one hand to another. It is a grey rook. The darkening queen is the "other" church, full of religious people accommodating all beliefs and doctrines, moving to grow its size by placing doctrine on the altar of sacrifice. It is the ecumenical "church" that takes on all comers. It is diversified and inclusive. Every belief system is under one roof. Native American medicine men, Buddhists, Muslims, Hindus, and others are welcome to come in and pray with the Christians. The dark queen grows darker and more powerful.

One day, this chessboard configuration will be blown off the table. Something will happen that re-establishes the pieces on both sides. This is a future event that is hard to predict. Perhaps it will be a <u>nuclear</u> explosion in a large, populated area. Only a handful of people are still with us today who were adults when Nagasaki and Hiroshima were devastated by the atomic bomb. And, while no one has ever witnessed the power, damage, and death that a nuclear explosion will produce, one can imagine the horrific aftermath of such a powerful weapon.

Thermonuclear bombs can be hundreds or even thousands of times more powerful than atomic bombs. The explosive yield of atomic bombs is measured in kilotons (one kiloton equals the explosive force of 1,000 tons of TNT) while the explosive power of thermonuclear bombs is frequently expressed in megatons (one megaton equals the explosive force of 1,000,000 tons of TNT).[158]

Imagine the outcry of the world for governments to come together to establish a super-government to prevent a future nuclear outbreak.[159]

After this world-shaking event, when the chessboard is re-established, there will be only one white piece remaining on the board: the king, Israel. The white queen, the church, will have disappeared. Vanished in the twinkling of the eye.[160] God will have removed His queen from the board.[161] **Israel will stand alone**.

---

[158] *Which is more powerful, a thermonuclear bomb or an atomic bomb?,* Encyclopedia Brittanica, May 25, 2024, https://www.britannica.com/question/Which-is-more-powerful-a-thermonuclear-bomb-or-an-atomic-bomb

[159] Paul the Apostle wrote of a prophetic outcry of people worldwide demanding peace and safety just prior to the great end-time event known as "The Day of the Lord" beginning. First Thessalonians 5:2-4 states: *"For you yourselves know full well that the day of the Lord is coming just like a thief in the night. ³ While they are saying, "Peace and safety!" then sudden destruction [h]will come upon them like labor pains upon a pregnant woman, and they will not escape."*

[160] The Apostle Paul wrote of this event in 1 Thessalonians 4:15-18: *"For we say this to you by the word of the Lord, that we who are alive [l]and remain until the coming of the Lord will not precede those who have fallen asleep. ¹⁶ For the Lord Himself will descend from heaven with a [m]shout, with the voice of the archangel and with the trumpet of God, and the dead in Christ will rise first. ¹⁷ Then we who are alive, who re-main, will be caught up together with them in the clouds to meet the Lord in the air, and so we will always be with the Lord. ¹⁸ Therefore, [n]com-fort one another with these words."* See also 1 Corinthians 15:52.

[161] See Author's Comments at the end of the chapter.

The dark pieces, thirteen of them, will have all become black with not a shade of grey, and they will be juxtaposed with the white king, Israel. The black king, Satan, will still stand as the ongoing enemy of Israel and know its vulnerability in the absence of the white church. Satan's once-darkening queen will have become deeply black. The black queen will appear as the apostate church, the spiritual entity of Satan, also known as the harlot in Revelation.[162] Ten of the remaining thirteen black pieces are very powerful nations (or kingdoms). These ten nations will be independent of each other but will meet to form the super-government that will rule over all governments of the world.

The last black piece on the board will be the little pawn – the one that seems so small as to be insignificant. In Scripture, this insignificant piece is a person known as the "Little Horn," also known as the antichrist! [163]

AUTHOR'S COMMENTS:

Comment 1 – **The Work of the Holy Spirit through the church, in both the forming of the State of Israel and protecting this country in world affairs:**

It is exciting for believers to realize that God employed the church as the primary driving force in the rebirth of the state of Israel. This event demonstrated the work of the Holy Spirit using individual believers in key positions in the world to bring about the fulfillment of a promise made to the Jews after they were dispersed throughout the world.

---

[162] See Revelation, Chapter 17

[163] See Daniel 7:8; 8:9-12; 9:27

> *Therefore behold, the days are coming," says the LORD, "that it shall no more be said, 'The LORD lives who brought up the children of Israel from the land of Egypt,' but, 'The LORD lives who brought up the children of Israel from the land of the north and from all the lands where He had driven them.' **For I will bring them back into their land which I gave to their fathers**."* (Jeremiah 16:14-15)

Well prior to the formation of the Jewish State of Israel in 1948, the Holy Spirit was actively moving the church to promote and support the formation of a Jewish homeland in Israel (Palestine). This was a movement known as Zionism. While Zionism was thought of as a movement originating from displaced Jews, it was actually Christians who initiated the concept and began the process that resulted in an official document produced by Great Britain. This document, known as the "Balfour Declaration," sanctioned the concept of a homeland for the Jews on the international stage.

> *Long before vague Jewish messianic aspirations became a concrete Zionist project, **and long before Jewish voices proclaimed Jews to be a nation rather than a religious group, Zionism was a <u>Christian venture</u>**. Zionism avant la letter, i.e. British proto-Zionism, emerged in the form of Christian Evangelical Restorationism, a movement calling for, and willing to sponsor, the emigration of Jews to Palestine as a precondition for the Second Coming of Christ (while simultaneously seeking to convert them to Christianity).*[164]

---

[164] Shafir, G. (2017, September 1). *Balfour 100 | Christian Zionism and the Balfour Declaration*. Fathom. Retrieved June 1, 2024, from https://fathomjournal.org/balfour-100-christian-zionism-and-the-balfour-declaration/

Arthur James Balfour was Prime Minister of the United Kingdom, and later, Great Britain's Foreign Secretary. In 1917, as Foreign Secretary, he authored and issued a letter on behalf of Great Britain known as the "Balfour Declaration." This declaration, which was the culmination of an ongoing Christian movement in England to restore the Jewish people to land in Palestine, aroused great hope among Zionists and partially fulfilled the aims of the World Zionist Organization.

> *A similar case was made at greater length by Sokolow in his magisterial History of Zionism 1600–1918, which appeared in 1919 with an introduction by Balfour. A significant part of this massive study is taken up with tracing the history of Christian Philosemitism and Restorationism in Britain. It presents* **the Balfour Declaration as the culmination of a long process that had gone on in the Christian world.**[165]

> *The declaration had many long-lasting consequences. It greatly increased popular support for* Zionism *within* Jewish communities worldwide, *and became a core component of the* British Mandate for Palestine, *the founding document of* Mandatory Palestine. **It indirectly led to the emergence of the** State of Israel *and is considered a principal cause of the ongoing* Israeli–Palestinian conflict, *often described as the world's most intractable conflict.*[166]

---

[165] Alexander, P. (2018, March 8). Why did Lord Balfour back the Balfour Declaration? *Jewish Historical Studies.* https://uclpress.scienceopen.com/hosted-document?doi=10.14324/111.444.jhs.2017v49.050
[166] Balfour Declaration. (2017, October 1). In *Wikipedia.* https://en.wikipedia.org/wiki/Balfour_Declaration

In 1948, The State of Israel was founded. The Holy Spirit then used Christians in influential roles to aid in the establishment and protection of the new nation. President Harry Truman, a Christian, firmly supported Israel's establishment as an independent state.

> *U.S. President Harry Truman was* **the first world leader to officially recognize Israel as a legitimate Jewish state on May 14, 1948, only eleven minutes after its creation.** *His decision came after much discussion and advice from the White House staff who had differing viewpoints. Some advisors felt that creating a Jewish state was the only proper response to the holocaust and would benefit American interests. Others took the opposite view, concerned about that the creation of a Jewish state would create more conflict in an already tumultuous region.*[167]

The example of the two Christians in key positions in governmental world affairs demonstrates how the Holy Spirit acts as a restraining force against evil through the church. When the church is removed from the earth, the Holy Spirit will also be removed[168] as an active power source against

---

[167] *Recognition of Israel.* National Archives - Truman Library. Retrieved June 1, 2024, from https://www.trumanlibrary.gov/education/presidential-inquiries/recognition-israel

[168] *"No one is to deceive you in any way! For it will not come unless the [d]apostasy comes first, and the man of lawlessness is revealed, the son of destruction, ⁴ who opposes and exalts himself above [e]every so-called god or object of worship, so that he takes his seat in the temple of God, displaying himself as being God. ⁵ Do you not remember that while I was still with you, I was telling you these things? ⁶ And you know what restrains him now, so that he will be revealed in his time. ⁷ For the mystery of lawlessness is already at work; only [f]He who now restrains will do so until [g]He is [h]removed"* (2 Thessalonians 2:3-7).

evil. While the Holy Spirit is omnipresent, He will no longer indwell people and lead them as He does the church today. After the removal of the church, a vacuum of evil will be created by its disappearance, accelerating the movement of the world toward the tribulation.

Comment 2 – **regarding the timing of the vanishing of the church**: there are three primary positions regarding an event known among Christians as the rapture, which is God's removal of the church from the earth. All three positions are stated in relation to a seven-year period on the earth known as "Daniel's 70th Week," or the tribulation. The opinion of the author is that the removal will occur prior to the start of the seven-year period, defined as the pre-tribulation rapture. The second position is the mid-tribulation rapture, which will take place at the 3 ½ year mark. The third is the post-tribulation rapture, which proponents say will occur at the end of the seven years. There is a position held by some church members that is a derivation of the mid-tribulation theory with a somewhat delayed timetable, known by its proponents as the pre-wrath rapture.

Comment 3 – **The 10-nation confederacy or "super-government."** *"Then I saw a beast coming up out of the sea, having ten horns and seven heads, and on his horns were ten crowns, and on his heads were blasphemous names"* (Revelation 13:1).

There are varying (and often weird) explanations given for this allegory, "The Beast." However, with careful study of the books of Daniel and Revelation, along with confirmation from studying and reading expository respected scholars in the field, the following conclusion seems to be the best interpretation of the allegory:

- A horn represents power in the Bible, and the crown on each horn represents a king or ruler of a powerful entity, likely a country.

- Six of the seven heads each represent an empire of history (with the seventh a future empire — the resurrected Roman Empire) that has treated/will treat Israel with evil. These seven empires are:

  - Egypt
  - Assyria
  - Babylon
  - Medo-Persia
  - Greece
  - Rome
  - Resurrected Rome – a future empire

- This beast is the seventh empire that will be a governmental system of ten nations (ten horns with ten crowns) with all the evil of the previous six empires in its action toward Israel. These ten nations will be loosely joined as a confederacy[169] but will function as the "super-government" and rule the world – for a time.

- The final iteration of the beast (the eighth) foresees the little horn arise and conquer or kill three of the horns (kings)

---

[169] Nebuchadnezzar's dream tells of ten toes made of a mixture of iron and clay, indicating that the union of the ten is loose and weak. See Daniel 2:41-43: *"Just as you saw that the feet and toes were partly of baked clay and partly of iron, so this will be a divided kingdom; yet it will have some of the strength of iron in it, even as you saw iron mixed with clay. [42] As the toes were partly iron and partly clay, so this kingdom will be partly strong and partly brittle. [43] And just as you saw the iron mixed with baked clay, so the people will be a mixture and will not remain united, any more than iron mixes with clay."*

and acquire their power. With this acquisition of power, the little horn (the antichrist) assumes world control.[170]

---

[170] *"After that, in my vision at night I looked, and there before me was a fourth beast—terrifying and frightening and very powerful. It had large iron teeth; it crushed and devoured its victims and trampled underfoot whatever was left. It was different from all the former beasts, and it had ten horns. [8] "While I was thinking about the horns, there before me was **another horn, a little one, which came up among them; and three of the first horns were uprooted before it**. This horn had eyes like the eyes of a human being and a mouth that spoke boastfully"* (Daniel 7:7-8).

Chapter 21

The Beast Rules

"One man's wickedness may easily become all men's curse."—
Publius Syrus

The chessboard has been reset. Satan will begin the match by moving pieces. One of his moves will ignite an explosive period of human suffering, destruction, and death of an intensity greater than the world has ever seen. It is a period known as the tribulation. This seven-year period is the outpouring of God's wrath upon the earth.[171] God's judgment and wrath have been withheld since the rejection of His Son two millennia ago. The execution of God's wrath in the tribulation consists of twenty-one separate judgments, in three groups of seven judgments each, being poured out upon the earth and the people who are alive during this time.

Preliminary to the tribulation, mankind will have changed the entire governmental landscape. This is the *New World*

---

[171] Some have speculated that the seven years of absolute devastation on the earth is some combination of man's wrath, followed by Satan's wrath, followed by God's wrath. While mankind's destructive force and Satan's demonic powers are evident during this time, all of these explosive displays during these seven years occur under the sovereignty of the Most High God. Each move, whether by man, Satan, or directly from God, is controlled by the opening of the seven-sealed scroll in heaven. It is the Lamb of God who breaks each seal, setting off the next judgment in the heaven-prescribed sequence. See Revelation 5:1-9.

Order that has been spoken of by world leaders.[172] In man's search for peace and safety, all nations will submit themselves to the rule of a super-government that consists of leaders (presidents, prime ministers, kings, and dictators) from ten selected nations. This group, this "Council-of-Ten"[173] will attempt to determine the course of all human activity and direction. The Council format of a 10-nation confederacy is yet another approach to self-government after man's repeated failure to rule himself.

Over forty years ago, Dr. Renald Showers, in the preface of his commentary on the book of Daniel, made this astounding statement:

> *Ironically, the more man tries to establish Utopia through self-rule the more his situation worsens. Instead of ruling the world in an orderly, meaningful way, he brings disorder, instability, and chaos. Man pollutes his environment. His world is shaken by wars and threats of war. His streets are filled with violence and crime. His economy becomes uncontrollable. He is gripped with the fear of total annihilation by his own doomsday weapons. He bruises the very institutions which have given society stability, order and direction. He is haunted by the prospect of death and the fear that life has no ultimate purpose or meaning.[174]*

---

[172] In March 1991, President George H. W. Bush addressed Congress at the end of the Gulf War in Iraq. In his speech, he outlined a "new world order" that would be **organized around the international communities' efforts** to halt aggression by the powerful over the powerless.

[173] *Council-of-Ten* is a term coined by the author. It is not a biblical term.

[174] Showers, R. E. (1982). *The Most High God* (10th ed.). Friends of Israel Gospel Ministry, Inc.

Forty-two years later, America's streets are far more violent; the richest country in the world moves rapidly ever closer to insolvency, and the threat of global war and mass destruction is more prevalent, while the cry for peace and safety at all costs grows louder.

This future Council-of-Ten is the beast of Revelation. The beast is a one-world government that has ten horns (of power) with ten crowns (rulers). This Council-of-Ten represents the re-generated empire of Rome. The Roman Empire once had worldwide power and exercised it by crushing every nation and people that stood against it. Such will be the force of the beast. It is Satan's government. It is a beast.

In parallel with the one-world rule of the beast is the harlot, Satan's religious system, a one-world religion that has merged all peoples' beliefs under one head. In ancient Rome's heyday, the head of their merged religions carried the title Pontifex Maximus, which was typically held by the emperor. The Pontifex Maximus was the chief priest, the final authority on religious law relating to the deities, and the "bridgebuilder to the gods."

> *In practice, particularly during the late Republic, the office of pontifex maximus was generally held by a member of a politically prominent family. It was a coveted position mainly for the great prestige it conferred on the holder. Julius Caesar became pontifex in 73 BC and pontifex maximus in 63 BC.*[175]

Satan's harlot, the one-world ecumenical "church," will be extremely powerful, bringing all religions in subjection to its authority. It will be diversified and accepting of all beliefs, that

---

[175] Pontifex maximus. (2024, May 29). In *Wikipedia*. https://en.wikipedia.org/wiki/Pontifex_maximus.

is, so long as there is tolerance and acceptance for all other belief systems under its umbrella of religious laws. Like Rome's
civil government, which crushes all opposition, the harlot will
persecute those who violate her dictates and directives. People
who discover Bibles, books and videos among their ruins and
believe on the Rescuer as the **only path to God** will be judged
as intolerable and find themselves in opposition to the harlot.[176]
They will be martyred for their faith.

> *When the Lamb broke the fifth seal, I saw underneath
> the altar the souls of those who had been killed because
> of the word of God, and because of the testimony which
> they had maintained.* (Revelation 6:9)

> *And I saw the woman* (The Harlot) *drunk with the
> blood of the saints, and with the blood of the witnesses
> of Jesus.* (Revelation 17:6)

This one-world church will have total authority to execute all
the new believers who hear the gospel message and stand in
opposition to the idols, false gods, and false message of peace
with God through multiple channels of belief. Because of its
control of the billions of religious followers world-wide, the
harlot will have great political influence over the Council-of-
Ten. Note in the passage below that the woman (the harlot) sits
on the beast, indicating that she will control the government's
direction. That she is intimate with the kings is an allegory of
the church's political bed-partnering with the rulers of the
world in order to achieve her objectives.

> *Then one of the seven angels who had the seven bowls
> came and spoke with me, saying, "Come here, I will
> show you the judgment of the great prostitute who sits*

---

[176] The true message of the gospel will also be brought to the unbelieving
world by 144,000 Jewish evangelists. Many will come to Christ through
their testimony. See Revelation chapters 7 and 14.

*on many waters, [2] with whom the kings of the earth committed acts of sexual immorality, and those who live on the earth became drunk with the wine of her sexual immorality." [3] And he carried me away [a] in the Spirit into a wilderness; and I saw a **woman sitting on a scarlet beast**, full of blasphemous names, having seven heads and ten horns.* (Revelation 17:1-3)

In the background, behind the operation of the harlot and the beast, is the one called the little horn. This is a man. Satan's man. He is likely European–possibly of Roman-Italian descent. He is called the little horn in Scripture for a reason. While he is a horn (powerful), he chooses to work in the shadows of the beast and the harlot. The little horn is the antichrist. He will be loved by the world. He is handsome, charismatic, a terrific spokesman, and he promotes peace. All the world loves a peacemaker.

As an advisor to, and representative of the beast, the ruling Council-of-Ten, the antichrist is sometimes looked upon as the 11th horn.[177] Little information is given in Revelation about Israel's ability to defend itself at the time that the antichrist makes his move, but it appears the Jews are in a bad way. Ever since the founding of the nation in 1948, this proud little nation's military has been considered one of the world's best. The soldiers have always been well-trained, dedicated, and armed with the highest technology, weapons, and equipment. The Iron Dome and David's Sling missile defenses have posted a tremendous battlefield track record defending itself from Arab, Iranian, and Palestinian missiles. When we see Israel in the future, it appears to be on its heels and standing alone against the world. The resupply of weapons from the United States will likely have been discontinued since America will be operating

---

[177] The term, *11th horn*, is one that some teachers use when studying Revelation Chapter 17. It is not a term used in Scripture.

under the authority of the beast. Perhaps Israel will have been weakened after having fought one of the end-time wars that have been prophesied but remain unfulfilled.[178]

When Israel appears to be on its heels, the peacemaker will move to broker a peace agreement with the nation and its people. This is the explosive charge that will ignite the world with a fire, which will burn for seven long years. The peacemaker will offer a seven-year ("week" of years) agreement that will guarantee Israel peace for that time period.

> *And he will confirm a covenant with the many for one week.*[179] (Daniel 9:27)

This is a curious move by the antichrist in following Satan's plan. Why would Satan ever want to protect the nation of Israel? The answer to this question lies in the Gospel of Matthew Chapter 23:

> *Jerusalem, Jerusalem, who kills the prophets and stones those who have been sent to her! How often I wanted to gather your children together, the way a hen gathers her chicks under her wings, and you were unwilling.* **38** *Behold, your house is being left to you desolate!* **39** *For I say to you, from now on* **you will not see Me until you say, 'Blessed is the One who comes in the name of the Lord!'"** (Matthew 23:37-39)

The Rescuer had just pronounced eight woes on the Pharisees in their confrontation with Him. After moving from that

---

[178] Two of these wars include the Ezekiel 38-39 War and the Psalm 83 War.

[179] The term, "week" was used in Daniel's day to describe a time period of seven. It could be seven days, seven weeks, seven years... In this case, it refers to seven years.

confrontation, He turned to the city, knowing the Jews' rejection of Him as Messiah, and announced the condition that must be fulfilled before He will return to claim His throne. The nation must recognize and accept Him as Messiah! The phrase "Blessed is He Who comes in the name of the Lord" is taken from a Messianic psalm, broadcasting the greeting of the Messiah.[180]

Satan, knowing that this is a condition for the return of the Rescuer, must stop the Jews from calling out to Him to return. To accomplish this, Satan must destroy Israel and the Jews. Satan and his antichrist also know that God will call all Jews back to Israel – a guarantee that He has made to restore the land to the people and return Jews to the land. The offering of a protective peace covenant to Israel will facilitate the return of all Jews to one area of the world, making it easier for the antichrist to destroy them. By destroying the nation and the people, the Rescuer will not return, and Satan's position as the god of the world will remain intact.

During the first 3 ½ years, the horror begins with the four horsemen "riding" to open the tribulation. The following paragraphs attempt to provide a thumbnail sketch of the events of each time segment:[181]

---

[180] *"Blessed is the one who comes in the name of the Lord; We have blessed you from the house of the Lord"* (Psalm 118:26).

[181] For a detailed study on the tribulation, I recommend the book by Theodore Epp, *Practical Studies in Revelation, Vol II.*, (Lincoln, Ne: The Good News Broadcasting Association, Inc., 1969.) It is out of print but can be found online in used bookstores.

In the first 3 ½ years

- Seven Seal Judgments[182] will be released from heaven. This is the first of three groups of seven judgments each, 21 total judgments in all.

- The white horse rider is the first seal judgment, which is symbolic of the peacemaker, the antichrist moving in power and guaranteeing Israel seven years of peace. Peace is short-lived. (Revelation 6:2)

- The red horse is the second seal judgment. It is symbolic of bloodshed from war – likely a massive nuclear war based on the number of the dead. (Revelation 6:3-4)

- The third seal judgment is the black horse, which is symbolic of the destruction, famine, and inflation that follow the war. (Revelation 6:5-6)

- The fourth, the pale horse, is symbolic of the awful toll of disease and death that follows the war. (Revelation 6:7-8)

- The fifth seal judgment speaks of the harlot who will persecute all the people who follow Christ as Savior. Since the church has been removed by the Holy Spirit, these people are often referred to as tribulation saints. Many will be executed for their faith. (Revelation 6:9-11)

- The sixth judgment is a devastating earthquake accompanied by supernatural activity in the atmosphere that will have never been seen before. These events will

---

[182] The seal judgments can be found in Revelation Chapter 6.

announce to the unbeliever, the agnostic, and the atheist that their world is under judgment. There will be a terrifying glimpse of the Most High God and His Son in the heavens, demonstrating the Creator God who is **the Sovereign** is authorizing these events. Judgment is underway! (Revelation 6:12-17)

- Twenty-five percent of the world's population will die during this period. Based on the current population estimate of the world, two billion people will lose their lives. (Revelation 6:8)

- The Jew, under the protection of the antichrist, will finally enjoy peace. Jews will be allowed to practice their religion, free from the persecution of the harlot. (It may be that it is the antichrist who will be instrumental in allowing the Jews to construct the third temple and restore their sacrificial system.)[183]

- Toward the end of the first half of the tribulation, the harlot, the idolatrous "church," will be destroyed by the Council-of-Ten (Revelation 17:16) and will move to consolidate civil and religious power under one head.[184]

---

[183] At the time of this writing, there is no temple for the Jews to reinstitute the sacrificial system. Daniel 9:27 speaks of the Jews' sacrifices being halted and the abomination in the Holy of Holies taking place. For the sacrifices and the abomination to occur and to have a Holy of Holies compartment, a third temple will have been constructed: *"And he will confirm a covenant with the many for one week, but in the middle of the week he will put a stop to **sacrifice and grain offering**; and on the wing of **abominations** will come the one who makes desolate."*

[184] *"And the ten horns which you saw, and the beast, these will hate the prostitute and will make her desolate and naked, and will eat her flesh and will burn her up with fire"* (Revelation 17:16).

Mid-Tribulation[185]

- During this mid-time, or in the months immediately prior to this time, the antichrist will move against three members of the Council-of-Ten, to eliminate them and acquire their power (Daniel 7:24). With the acquisition of this power the antichrist will assume total control of the Council (Revelation 17:17) and total control of the world. It is at this time that the governmental structure will morph into its final form. Because the antichrist will be in total control, the term "the beast" can refer to the governmental system or the antichrist. In a sense, they are one and the same.[186]

- The antichrist's false prophet[187] will enter the temple of the Jews and then the Holy of Holies – a place reserved for the Most High God. The false prophet will place an image of the antichrist demanding that it be worshipped (Revelation 13:14-15). As Lucifer said, "I will be as the Most High God." (2Thessalonians 2:4)

- At this mid-tribulation mark, the antichrist will break the peace agreement with the Jews and become the worst persecutor of Jews the world has ever seen.[188] He

---

[185] See Revelation chapters 13 & 17 and Daniel chapters 7 & 9 for more detail concerning these events.

[186] When the term "beast," is used in Scripture, it can refer to either the antichrist, the governmental system, or both. It is important to study the context in which the term is *being* used to determine if it is the government, or the antichrist, or both that are being referred to.

[187] The false prophet is a man who becomes the religious promoter of the antichrist after the destruction of the harlot. See Revelation 13:11-17

[188] *"Therefore when you see the abomination of desolation which was spoken of through Daniel the prophet, standing in the holy place—[k]let*

will move to annihilate all of Abraham's offspring so that no Jew will be able to cry out to the Rescuer to return as their Messiah. (Matthew 24:15-21)

- With the destruction of the harlot, the idolatrous church, all idol worship ceases. The antichrist demands that he, and he alone, is worshipped. (Revelation 13:15-16)

- Worldwide, all people will be required to receive the mark of the beast. This mark will be necessary to work, buy food, receive and spend money. This mark will also serve as a sign of worship. (Revelation 13:16-17)

In the second 3 ½ years[189]

- The opening of the last seal judgment (the 7th seal) will open the seven trumpet judgments in sequence. (Revelation 8:1)

- The first four trumpet judgments will be environmental in nature and result in bloody rivers and oceans, massive fish kills, sunken shipping vessels, worldwide fires and other calamities. This judgment will pollute

---

the [l]reader understand— [16] then those who are in Judea must flee to the mountains. [17] [m]Whoever is on the [n]housetop must not go down to get things out of his house. [18] And [o]whoever is in the field must not turn back to get his cloak. [19] But woe to those women who are pregnant, and to those who are nursing babies in those days! [20] Moreover, pray that [p]when you flee, it will not be in the winter, or on a Sabbath. [21] For then there will be a great tribulation, such as has not occurred since the beginning of the world until now, nor ever will again" (Matthew 24:15-21).

[189] See Revelation chapters 8 and 9 for the trumpet judgments, and Revelation Chapter 16 for the bowl judgments.

drinking water and destroy food from the sea. (Revelation 8:7-13)

- The fifth and sixth trumpet judgments will be demonic. They will unleash two waves of demons. The first wave will inflict horrible pain on all who carry the mark of the beast, but the demons will not allow the sufferers to die. The second wave of 200 million demons kills one-third of the world's population. Two additional billion people die. Since the beginning of the tribulation, over half of the world's population will have perished. (Revelation 9:1-18)

- The seventh trumpet will open the seven bowl judgments, which are the most severe of all judgments. There will be seven bowls of wrath poured out directly from heaven, in sequence (Revelation 16:1-17). Jesus said these judgments will be so intense that if He does not cut them short, no one on Earth will live to the end of the tribulation.[190]

As the end of the tribulation approaches, during the bowl judgment, the antichrist will make a call to the countries of the world under his command to assemble for the final battle. Note that the assembly will include his demon army.

> *And I saw coming out of the mouth of the dragon, and out of the mouth of the beast, and out of the mouth of the false prophet, three unclean spirits like frogs; ¹⁴ for they are spirits of demons, performing signs, which go out to the kings of the entire* [g]*world, to gather them*

---

[190] "*And if those days had not been cut short, no life would have been saved; but for the sake of the elect those days will be cut short.* [See Revelation Chapter 16 for the bowl judgments.]" (Matthew 24:22).

together for the war of the great day of God, the Almighty. (Revelation 16:13-14)

Satan's armies of the world of untold size will gather in mass along a 120-mile front from Jerusalem north to a hill called Har-Magedon,[191] (Hill of Megiddo) to Bozrah to the southeast of Jerusalem. There will be a massive assault on the city of Jerusalem to open the battle of Armageddon. A remnant of Jews (one-third of the Jews that remain alive[192]) will recognize that the One who they rejected and crucified is their Messiah, and they will cry out to Him as their Savior.[193]

With the cry of the remnant, the return of the Rescuer will be set in motion. Jesus the Christ, the Messiah of Israel and the world, will return and confront Satan, the antichrist, his false prophet, all of Satan's demons, and the human armies of the world. Revelation Chapter 19 describes this astounding and glorious event:

> *And I saw heaven opened, and behold, a white horse, and He who sat on it is called Faithful and True, and in righteousness He judges and wages war. 12 His eyes are a flame of fire, and on His head are many crowns; and He has*

---

[191] It is from the name of this mount or hill that the name of Armageddon is derived.

[192] *"And it will come about in all the land,"* declares the Lord, *"That two parts in it will be cut off and perish; **but the third will be left in it.** 9 And I will bring the third part through the fire, refine them as silver is refined, And test them as gold is tested. **They will call on My name, And I will answer them; I will say, 'They are My people,' And they will say, 'The Lord is my God'"** (Zechariah 13:8-9).

[193] *"And I will pour out on the house of David and on the inhabitants of Jerusalem the Spirit of **grace and of pleading,** so that **they will look at Me whom they pierced;** and they will mourn for Him, like one mourning for an only son, and they will weep bitterly over Him like the bitter weeping over a firstborn"* (Zechariah 12:10).

a name written on Him which no one knows except Himself. [13] He is clothed with a robe dipped in blood, and His name is called The Word of God. [14] And the armies which are in heaven, clothed in fine linen, white and clean, were following Him on white horses. [15] From His mouth comes a sharp sword, so that with it He may strike down the nations, and He will rule them with a rod of iron; and He treads the wine press of the fierce wrath of God, the Almighty. [16] And on His robe and on His thigh He has a name written: "KING OF KINGS, AND LORD OF LORDS." (Revelation 19:11-16)

The army that returns with the Rescuer includes His angelic host of heaven and His church (all believers (*clothed in fine linen, white and clean* – a picture of those saved by grace)) – those who were removed from the earth (raptured) prior to the start of the tribulation.)

The battle lines have been drawn for Armageddon …

Chapter 22

God With Us

"The God who has promised a better world is the God who cannot lie. He will shake loose Satan's hold on this world and its society and systems. Our heavenly Father will put this world into the hands that were once nailed to a cross for our race of proud and alienated sinners."—A.W. Tozer

For thousands of years, Satan has been weaving his underground wiring of idolatry, the façade of religious systems, evil business practices, economic booby traps, and political poison. Much like a theme park, *SatanWorld*, with its city-beneath-the-city, has run the show above. His operator-demons have monitored and adjusted humanity's society and practices to the delight of the park's owner. Billions of people have visited this world-wide park on a daily basis and have been delighted to have ridden through the exciting experience. It so satisfies the inner, fallen man.

Over the seven years of the tribulation, *SatanWorld* will be slowly dismantled. The bombardment of the nuclear seal judgments, followed by the increasingly destructive and death-rendering trumpet judgments, and then the even-worse pouring of the acid wrath from the bowl judgments of heaven will have Satan, the antichrist, the false prophet and the demons on their heels. Half of the human population will be dead. Gone. Nothing will function properly according to the design of its master, Satan.

> *And I saw the beast and the kings of the earth and their armies, assembled to make war against Him who sat on the horse, and against His army.*
> (Revelation 19:19)

The armies of the world will be assembled and positioned for a once-and-for-all battle with the armies of the Rescuer. Satan, his demons, the antichrist, and the false prophet will be confident. They will have massed the troops that have controlled the world for the past seven years, despite these judgments from heaven. Satan will manipulate his underlings and himself with his lies. They will all believe that victory will be theirs. After all, doesn't the name Satan mean the deceiver? He will even deceive himself!

The antichrist and the armies of the world will have already begun the attack. The assault on Jerusalem with overwhelming numbers will attempt to destroy all Jews in the city. By engaging the city and the land to their west, they will attempt to sweep through the territory from the east of the Jordan, west to the Mediterranean, *from the River to the Sea.*[194] These evil forces will try to consolidate their position to the west, behind them. In parallel, all remaining forces will dig in facing the anticipated onslaught of the Rescuer and his army that will come from the east.

Although the battle line will extend 120 miles from Bozrah through Jerusalem and north to the Mount of Megiddo, the pinnacle of the confrontation will be centered on Jerusalem, in the valley of Jehoshaphat, also identified as the Valley of Decision, the area between the Mount of Olives and Mount Zion.

---

[194] This was the antisemitic cry of the world following the October 7, 2023 killing spree of Hamas on Israel.

As the city is being overrun[195], the cry of *the Remnant*[196] will go up to the heavens,[197] the Rescuer will descend to the same location that he ascended from, the Mount of Olives. [198]

With His army from heaven behind Him, the Rescuer will view the impressive army that was assembled by the anti-christ. Both he and the false prophet are their supreme leaders. They stand proudly, well out in front of the soldiers assembled to battle so that they are clearly visible.

Just prior to the opening of this final battle, an angel will assemble the birds to feast on the flesh of the dead that will quickly come. The birds will be there in masse! Israel has the largest flyway in the world for migrating birds. Over 500,000,000 birds migrate through the area annually.[199]

---

[195] *"Behold, a day is coming for the Lord when the spoils taken from you will be divided among you. ² For I will gather all the nations against Jerusalem to battle, and the city will be taken, the houses plundered, the women raped, and half of the city exiled, but the rest of the people will not be eliminated from the city"* (Zechariah 14:1-2).

[196] The one-third part of the Jews alive at the end of the tribulation as spoken of in Zechariah 13:9.

[197] *"You will not see Me until you say, 'Blessed is the One who comes in the name of the Lord!'"* This is the cry that will go up to the heavens in which the remnant of Jews will finally recognize the crucified Jesus as their Messiah" (Matthew 23:39).

[198] *"Then the Lord will go forth and fight against those nations, as when He fights on a day of battle. ⁴ On that day His feet will stand on the Mount of Olives, which is in front of Jerusalem on the east; and the Mount of Olives will be split in its middle from east to west forming a very large valley"* (Zechariah 14:3-4).

[199] Blackburn, N. (2009, March 30). *TAKING WING AT THE LARGEST FLYWAY IN THE WORLD*. Israel 21c. Retrieved June 9, 2024, from https://www.israel21c.org/taking-wing-at-the-largest-flyway-in-the-world/

*Then I saw an angel standing in the sun, and he cried
out with a loud voice, saying to all the birds that fly
in midheaven, "Come, assemble for the great feast of
God,* [18] *so that you may eat the flesh of kings and the
flesh of commanders, the flesh of mighty men, the
flesh of horses and of those who sit on them, and the
flesh of all people, both free and slaves, and small
and great"* (Revelation 19:17-18)

Scripture gives a very short description of the line of battle.

*And I saw the beast and the kings of the earth and
their armies, assembled to make war against Him
who sat on the horse, and against His army.* (Revelation 19:19)

Like opposing leaders, the Rescuer, sitting on His majestic
white stallion, will be positioned well in front of His army.
The Christ versus the antichrist. The attack begins, initiated
by the Rescuer. Instead of commanding His troops into battle, only the Rescuer moves forward. His army will not participate in the battle. They will observe because they are not
needed. Why help the omnipotent One? It is the power of the
Word of God, the sharp sword that comes from the mouth of
the Rescuer, that will obliterate His opposition.

Normally, in battle, there is great conflict between the troops
of the opposing sides; a victor emerges, taking prisoners
from the defeated army. But not in this battle. In a stunning
move, the first action in the confrontation will be the omnipotent Christ crossing the Valley of Decision and taking the
antichrist and his prophet into captivity. Satan's army will
do nothing, because they can do nothing. They will remain
frozen in their foxholes while they watch the judgment and
execution of their leaders.

And the beast was seized, and with him the false prophet who performed the signs in his presence, by which he deceived those who had received the mark of the beast and those who worshiped his image; these two were thrown alive into the lake of fire, which burns with brimstone. (Revelation 19:20)

With the antichrist and his false prophet captured and judgment executed, the Sovereign Rescuer, the Christ, will turn His eyes of fire onto the warring army opposing Him. With one Word from the omnipotent, living Word of God, the army is destroyed.

And the rest were killed with the sword which came from the mouth of Him who sat on the horse, and all the birds were filled with their flesh. (Revelation 19:21)

The prophecy of Zechariah provides more detail of this action. His one word will cover the entire army position across the 120-mile front. It will be like a plague upon mankind when He strikes:

Now this will be the plague with which the Lord will strike all the peoples who have gone to war against Jerusalem; their flesh will rot while they stand on their feet, and their eyes will rot in their sockets, and their tongue will rot in their mouth. 13 And it will come about on that day that a great panic from the Lord will fall on them; and they will seize one another's hand, and the hand of one will be raised against the hand of another. (Zechariah 14:12-13)

It will be all over in a moment. There will be no POWs. None.

Immediately after the battle, the victorious Christ will march into Jerusalem and proceed to Mount Zion. There, waiting for Him, will be the 144,000 Jews – 12,000 men from each of the twelve tribes. After the church will be removed prior to these end-time events, the evangelical baton that was taken from Israel and given to the church almost 2,000 years prior will be given back to these faithful believers of Abraham's seed. For seven long years, these Jews will have gone out to the world, carrying the gospel message of their soon-coming King.

With His victory, they will gather around Him, first in worship, then in joyful celebration.[200] Afterward, they will lead Him to David's throne. There, they will crown Him with many crowns. The Davidic Covenant will finally be fulfilled! The Lion of the Tribe of Judah will take His rightful seat on Israel's throne!

The word will spread quickly. The people of faith who refused the *mark of the beast* and somehow escaped death, will come out of hiding. Even with all the death and destruction from the seven-year outpouring of God's wrath and the bloodletting from the recently completed battle of Armageddon, these tribulation saints will be joyous and full of hope. The King they will have placed their faith in—the One they will have trusted to save them—will now sit on the throne. From that throne, He will rule the world.

---

[200] *"Then I looked, and behold, the Lamb was standing on Mount Zion, and with Him 144,000 who had His name and the name of His Father written on their foreheads. ² And I heard a voice from heaven, like the sound of many waters and like the sound of loud thunder, and the voice which I heard was like the sound of harpists playing on their harps. ³ And they *sang a new song before the throne and before the four living creatures and the elders; and no one was able to learn the song except the 144,000 who had been purchased from the earth"* (Revelation 14:1-3)

And then there is Satan – the defeated one. The King will immediately dispatch an angel from heaven. The disposition of the Devil is recorded in the book of Revelation:

> *Then I saw an angel coming down from heaven, holding the key of the abyss and a great chain in his hand. [2] And he took hold of the dragon, the serpent of old, who is the devil and Satan, and bound him for a thousand years; [3] and he threw him into the abyss and shut it and sealed it over him, so that he would not deceive the nations any longer, until the thousand years were completed; after these things he must be released for a short time.*[201] (Revelation 20:1-3)

With the King on His throne and the capture and disposition of Satan, a new age will have begun. The first day of world peace will be welcomed by the world. The god of this world will have been dethroned, and the God of Creation, the Most High God, the King of kings and Lord of lords, the Alpha and the Omega, David's son, and the Son of God will now rule the world. There will be true and lasting peace on the earth. All weapons of warfare will be turned into productive tools of prosperity.

This King will rule like no one else could, for He is God and has all the attributes of God. He is all-knowing, all-powerful, and all-present. It is the King with these characteristics who will rule the nations. He is the true super-government. He is a theocracy! Man has tried to govern himself for thousands of years with no recognition of the Most High. All attempts to administer lasting worldwide peace through superpowers, the League of Nations, and the United Nations have failed

---

[201] Yes. Satan will be released, but only after the 1000-year reign of Jesus Christ. Satan's release will be temporary, after which, he will be thrown into the lake of fire for eternity.

miserably. The record of death and destruction that is the by-product of their rule tells the story.

In the end, it will be evident to all. The throne was just too big for Satan. He just couldn't measure up. He could never, and will never be …

THE ANGEL WHO WOULD BE GOD!

BIBLIOGRAPHY

(2024). The New American Standard Bible. Bible Gateway. Retrieved July 7, 2024, from https://www.biblegateway.com/

(1984). Studies in Church History, Volume 21: Persecution and Toleration (pp. 51-72). W.J. Sheils, Editor.

Alexander, P. (2018, March 8). Why did Lord Balfour back the Balfour Declaration? Jewish Historical Studies. Retrieved July 7, 2024, from https://uclpress.scienceopen.com/hosted-document?doi=10.14324/111.444.jhs.2017v49.050

Balfour Declaration. (2017, October 1). In Wikipedia. Retrieved July 7, 2024, from https://en.wikipedia.org/wiki/Balfour_Declaration

Barnhouse, D. (1970). Genesis (p. 48). Grand Rapids, MI: Zondervan Publishing Company.

Bible Affirming Truth. DAVID AND GOLIATH. One Page. Retrieved May 16, 2024, from https://www.onepagebiblesummary.com/bat/bat_05.php

Biological Warfare. Wikipedia. Retrieved May 15, 2024, from https://en.wikipedia.org/wiki/Biological_warfare

Blackburn, N. (2009, March 30). TAKING WING AT THE LARGEST FLYWAY IN THE WORLD. Israel 21c. Retrieved June 9, 2024, from https://www.israel21c.org/taking-wing-at-the-largest-flyway-in-the-world/

Butler, R. (1979). The Black Angels. New York: St. Martin's Press.

Carlin, L. (2016, August 23). Babylon, the mother of all false religions. Ag Air Update.

Collins, L., & Lapierre, D. (1988). O Jerusalem. New York: Simon & Schuster.

Defining Antisemitism. U.S. Department of State. Retrieved October 22, 2024, from https://www.state.gov/defining-antisemitism/

Dien Bien Phu & the Fall of French Indochina, 1954. Office of the Historian, US Department of State. Retrieved May 12, 2024, from https://history.state.gov/milestones/1953-1960/dien-bien-phu#:~:text=In%20early%201954%2C%20the%20French,links%20on%20the%20Laotian%20border.

Epp, T. H. (1969). Practical Studies in Revelation, Vol II. Lincoln, NE: The Good News Broadcasting Association, Inc.

"Genesis 3 – The Fall – Why did Adam Sin?", Revealed Truth, 2024. Retrieved October 22, 2024, from https://www.revealedtruth.com/bible-study/genesis3-adam-sin-fall/

Ghost Army: The Combat Con Artists of World War II. National WWII Museum. Retrieved May 9, 2024, from https://www.nationalww2museum.org/visit/exhibits/traveling-exhibits/ghost-army-combat-con-artists-world-war-ii

Herod King of Judea. Encyclopedia Britannica. Retrieved May 6, 2024, from https://www.britannica.com/biography/Herod-king-of-Judaea

Holden, M. (2012, September 3). God Did Not Create the Universe, says Hawking. Reuters. Retrieved May 10, 2024, from https://www.reuters.com/article/idUSTRE6811FN/

Iwo Jima and Okinawa: Death at Japan's Doorstep. National WWII Museum. Retrieved May 15, 2024, from https://www.nationalww2museum.org/war/articles/iwo-jima-and-okinawa-death-japans-doorstep

Japanese propaganda leaflet recovered during the Battle of Okinawa. Naval History and Heritage Command. Retrieved May 15, 2024, from https://www.history.navy.mil/content/history/nhhc/our-collections/artifacts/ephemera/letters/japanese-propaganda-leaflet--battle-of-okinawa.html

Macbeth, Act 4, Scene 1.A play by William Shakespeare. Retrieved October 22, 2024, from https://www.folger.edu/explore/shakespeares-works/macbeth/read/4/1/

McDowell, J. (1981). The Resurrection Factor (p. 56). San Bernardino, CA: Here's Life Publishers

Milton, J. (2024). Paradise Lost, Book IV [The Argument]. Poets.org. Retrieved July 7, 2024, from https://poets.org/poem/paradise-lost-book-iv-argument

Milton, J. (2024). Paradise Lost Quotes. Goodreads. Retrieved July 7, 2024, from https://www.goodreads.com/work/quotes/1031493-paradise-lost

Mishal, N. (2008). Israel 60 - Those Were The Years (p. 17). Tel-Aviv: Miskal-Publishing and Distribution, Ltd.

Moran, F. (n.d.). History of Jewish Persecution | Antisemitism, Reasons & Problems. Study.com. Retrieved

October 22, 2024, from https://study.com/academy/lesson/history-of-jewish-persecution.html

Moses and Pharaoh. Encyclopedia Britannica. Retrieved May 12, 2024, from https://www.britannica.com/biography/Moses-Hebrew-prophet/Moses-and-Pharaoh

Pontifex maximus. (2024, May 29). In Wikipedia. Retrieved July 7, 2024, from https://en.wikipedia.org/wiki/Pontifex_maximus

Recognition of Israel. National Archives - Truman Library. Retrieved June 1, 2024, from https://www.trumanlibrary.gov/education/presidential-inquiries/recognition-israel

Shafir, G. (2017, September 1). Balfour 100 | Christian Zionism and the Balfour Declaration. Fathom. Retrieved June 1, 2024, from https://fathomjournal.org/balfour-100-christian-zionism-and-the-balfour-declaration/

Showers, R. E. (1982). The Most High God (10th ed.). Bellmawr, NJ: Friends of Israel Gospel Ministry, Inc.

Smith, B. L. (1999, July 26). Propaganda. Encyclopedia Britannica. Retrieved May 15, 2024, from https://www.britannica.com/topic/propaganda

The History of Biological Warfare. (n.d.). Retrieved May 12, 2024, from https://www.ncbi.nlm.nih.gov/pmc/articles/PMC1326439/

The History of Biological Warfare, Friedrich Frischknecht, EMBO Reports, June, 2003.

UN General Assembly condemns Israel 14 times in 2023, rest of world 7. U.N. Watch. Retrieved May 26, 2024, from https://unwatch.org/un-general-assembly-condemns-israel-14-times-in-2023-rest-of-world-7/#:~:text=NEW%20YORK%2C%20December%2020%2C%202023,rest%20of%20the%20world%20combined.

Unger, M. F. (1957). Unger's Bible Dictionary (3rd ed., p. 115). Chicago, IL: Moody Press.

Questions. Retrieved May 10, 2024, from https://www.got-questions.org/star-of-Bethlehem.html

Which is more powerful, a thermonuclear bomb or an atomic bomb? Encyclopedia Britannica. Retrieved May 25, 2024, from https://www.britannica.com/question/Which-is-more-powerful-a-thermonuclear-bomb-or-an-atomic-bomb

Zavada, J. (2019, December 4). Biblical History of Ancient Babylon. Learn Religions. Retrieved May 5, 2024, from https://www.learnreligions.com/history-of-babylon-3867031

SCRIPTURE INDEX

	11:47-48	124
	11:49-52	129
	11:53	124
	13:26-27	129
	13:31-32	83
	14:6	136
	19:28	116
Acts	1:6-8	149
	2:1-3	148
Romans	3:23	136
	4:25	134
	8:1	148
	8:6-8	32
	8:22	32
1 Corinthians	5:5	40
	6:15-16	82
	10:20	90
	15:12-19	142
	15:14-19	134
	15:52	172
2 Corinthians	4:3-4	x,29,31,37,120
Ephesians	1:3-5	118
	1:4	34
	1:13	148
	2:2	19
	2:8-9	74
Philippians	2:5-8	115
Colossians	2:9	15

213